Homeless.
Hope!

A solution to the affordable housing crisis in the South-west

A prospectus for community cohesion, affordable housing and economic prosperity for the South-West peninsula

DaCSTaR ® Devon and Cornwall Sustainable Travel and Regeneration

"And those young twins,

Free Thought and clean Fresh Air:

Attend the long express from Waterloo

That takes us down to Cornwall. Tea-time shows

The small fields waiting, every blackthorn hedge

Straining inland before the south-west gale.

The emptying train, wind in the ventilators,

Puffs out of Egloskerry to Tresmeer

Through minty meadows, under bearded trees

And hills upon whose sides the clinging farms

Hold Bible Christians. Can it really be

That this same carriage came from Waterloo?

On Wadebridge station what a breath of sea

Scented the Camel valley! Cornish air,

Soft Cornish rains, and silence after steam..."

Sir John Betjeman "Summoned by Bells"

DaCSTaR ®   Devon and Cornwall Sustainable Travel and Regeneration

DaCSTaR ® Devon and Cornwall Sustainable Travel and Regeneration

Homeless. Helpless! Hopeless?

A prospectus for community cohesion, affordable housing and economic prosperity for the South-West peninsula.

Published by Mainsail Voyages Press Ltd, Hartland Forest Golf Club, Bideford, Devon, EX39 5RA.

ISBN-13 9798390360071
Text typeset in Calibri 12 point

All historical map excerpts are reproduced with the permission of the National Library of Scotland.
Almost all photographs are courtesy of Bernard Mills; all exceptions are individually acknowledged.

DaCSTaR ®   Devon and Cornwall Sustainable Travel and Regeneration

Contents

	page
Introduction	1
What is **DaCSTaR**?	13
Caveats: technical, research, financial	15
What is the fundamental mechanism to achieve the stated objectives?	18
Why is a railway restoration an essential element of this scheme?	31
Is this the time to contemplate such an investment when the UK economy is facing difficult challenges?	35
But how could a modern-day railway succeed when Dr Beeching closed lines which were extremely unprofitable?	38
The lost railways: What happened?	40
The lost lines: Where were they? Who did they serve?	48
The maximum potential for restoration of lost railway lines	49
The network schema	52
The lost lines: Who might they serve, if restored?	56
Restoration: Lost causes? A pipe dream or not?	60
The present state of track-beds, bridges, tunnels, obstructions, alternatives	65
The lost lines: trains, stations and halts, length of lines, potential users, timetables	67
The Ilfracombe to Barnstaple Line: an example of a restored railway line.	75
A bridge across the River Taw	79
The Lynton to Barnstaple Line: an example of a restored railway line.	84
The Devon and Somerset Railway - Taunton to Barnstaple	93
The Exe Valley Railway	100
Halwill Junction: key junction for northern Devon and north Cornwall	107
Halwill Junction to Bude	112
Halwill Junction to Launceston	116
Wadebridge	120

DaCSTaR ®   Devon and Cornwall Sustainable Travel and Regeneration

Contents (continued)

	page
Padstow	123
Tavistock	130
Tariffs and passenger payment	140
The economic benefits of restoration: illustrations	148
The social benefits of restoration: illustrations	149
Downsides: are there any?	151
The costs of restoration	152
A brief and simplistic summary:	157
What kind of trains would suit? A return to steam?	159
Restored lines, stations and halts: a new, simpler format	165
Historical station (platform) layouts:	168
Alternative station (platform) layouts:	170
Proposed railway lines and platforms at Barnstaple Junction:	173
Proposed railway lines and platforms at a new Halwill Junction station:	176
Essential and desirable station services:	178
The costs of operation: How could such be affordable?	180
Ownership: Who would own the lines?	182
The preservation of existing (and potentially future) walking & cycling trails	193
The legal necessities and the Law: an Enabling mechanism	195
The Transport and Works Act 1992	196
Appropriation of land for the programme	197
Opposition: mechanisms to overcome such	202
HM Government support for railway restoration	204
Invitation: Contribute, correct, share, distribute, contact	209
Appendix: Recommended books on the 'lost' railway lines of the region	211

Introduction

The South-West peninsula of Devon and Cornwall, more specifically its rural regions, has long endured almost the lowest GDP *per capita* within the UK. For example, Torridge District in northern Devon, the poorest of Devon's districts, has a lower GDP than even the Outer Hebrides and the Shetland Islands.

The economic trials and ills of **Cornwall**, in particular, are well known; they are described in many papers produced by both Local Government authors and the press. Such documents are an excellent source of information on the subject, which needs no repetition or elaboration within this document. However, it is worth succinctly stating a very few of such significant aspects of concern for the county:

- Cornwall has a GDP which is only two-thirds of the national average*, with a high proportion of employment being low paid and seasonal; indeed, Cornwall has almost the lowest wages of all UK regions;

- It was reported that in 2016 in north Cornwall 42% of employees earned *below the living wage*; in south east Cornwall the figure was 39%*;

- Average remuneration in Cornwall in 2019 was £19,763 (79% of the UK average) *

   * *source:*
https://www.theguardian.com/business/2020/mar/04/levelling-up-britain-why-cornwall-needs-more-than-just-tourism

- Many more people every year opt to live in Cornwall, increasing the population and pushing up demand for services such as GP surgeries, hospitals, schools, roads, housing and utilities. Demand is highest in coastal and estuary areas, boosting house prices to those usually found in the relatively more prosperous UK south-east;

- HM Government funding for housing is miniscule in absolute terms, perhaps funding about circa twenty homes per annum; such does not scratch the surface of the county's most challenging problem: the lack of affordable housing for the indigenous population;

- 23,000 households are on the waiting list for council housing, yet there are only 10,000 council homes in Cornwall;
- There are an estimated 10,000 holiday-lets plus 13,000 second homes in the county, 23,000 properties in all;
- The council spends £40,000 per day (£14.6 million p.a.) on emergency accommodation;
- Even shipping containers are being installed on council car parks for homeless people to live in. *How extreme do things have to become?***

** source: *https://www.telegraph.co.uk/property/buy-to-let/local-teachers-cant-find-home-holiday-let-owner-local-councillor/*

In Devon the situation is scarcely different; for example: it has been reported that one in eight children in the county live in poverty, and one in three children in parts of Barnstaple (the Forches Estate) do so.

Constant inward migration is pushing up house prices in Devon, making the affordability of a home increasingly precarious for the indigenous population.

Fuel poverty and poor housing quality are endemic problems in north and west Devon (and also in areas of Cornwall too), and - *significantly* - this was *before* the massive 2022 energy price rises.

In everyday life the general lack of under-investment and the economic deprivation within both Devon and Cornwall translates (amongst many criteria) to the long-recognised crisis of a lack of affordable housing. In the predominantly rural areas, public transportation is also very poor. **Torridge District**, to illustrate one example, has no rail link to anywhere.

The regional 'capital' of northern Devon, Barnstaple, has one rail line to Exeter, one of only two cities in Devon. Of course, further afield the mainline railway from the rest of the UK to the north-east, and to the south-west as far as the SW extremity of Cornwall at Penzance, still exists; but aside from a very few branch lines in the south and south-west of the Counties (to St. Ives, Gunnislake, Looe, Exmouth *etc*) the branch railways of Devon and Cornwall have been nigh on wholly expunged since sixty years ago.

The arrival of the railways in the mid-nineteenth century was everywhere greeted with joy by local populations who - for the most part - had never before travelled more than a few miles from home and *by horse*. Only the more affluent could afford the stage coach, and that was such an uncomfortable experience, on dreadful roads, that few embraced the prospect with pleasure.

As the railways reached their heyday in the 1930s after a relatively short period of 60 years of almost exponential growth, the writing was already on the wall: the internal combustion engine (ICE), in the form of the car, was about to arrive. That has been one of the marvels of human invention, facilitating travel for all (at least in the UK and the developed world); yet even now, a mere 90 years later, the *electric* car is about to succeed its internal combustion engine predecessor.

However, such electric vehicles are, relative to the ICE-car, *expensive*; to the extent that they remain at present unaffordable to the majority of households in the south-west. "Old Bangers" are set to endure for some considerable time to come.

Even so, it is reported* (at the time of writing, in November 2022) that 40% of car owners will require help to simply stay on the road; a transition to an electric vehicle is clearly beyond their resources. That percentage may be even higher in the south-west.

* source https://www.telegraph.co.uk/money/consumer-affairs/half-drivers-need-financial-support-keep-cars-road/

In terms of **housing**, which is possibly the greatest problem facing society in the region, the situation is acutely difficult for families living in rented accommodation. In some regions of the peninsula the proportion of homes being second homes is extremely substantial; so much so that it exerts an undesirable and depressive influence upon local communities, depriving local people of a home; most particularly so the youngest members of communities. In discrete and popular parts of North Devon the proportion of second homes approaches a staggering 50%!

Furthermore, in **North Devon** the proportion of second homes or of long-term *empty* homes which do <u>not</u> have a statutory exemption from council tax* is one in every 21 properties, while in East Devon it's one in every 23, in Torridge it's one in every 24, and in West Devon it's one in every 34. It is part of an undesirable trend termed *"buy to leave"*, which is the purchase of a property which is subsequently left empty (without any perceived 'hassle' from tenants or holidaymakers) in the expectation that the value of it will rise. *

* source: https://www.devonlive.com/news/property/numbers-second-homes-devon-continue-7833683 (well worth reading)

Some properties, whether occupied or not occupied, are exempt from council tax. For example, these include uninhabitable properties requiring or undergoing repair, or the occupier has died, the occupier has moved to a care home or is in hospital or in prison etc.

The housing crisis within Devon and Cornwall is severe by any standard; so much so that Torridge District Council, at the start of 2023, 'launched' a well-intentioned and laudable discussion for housing refugees in a cruise vessel, rather than in any other land accommodation - *because there is none available at all.* In fact, one in 279 people within Torridge are homeless, the District plight being the worst within Devon and Cornwall;

* source: https://www.bbc.co.uk/news/uk-england-devon-64234515

This remarkable proposition (since rejected) and the BBC article in which it was described merits comment on several points:

1. The housing crisis within the UK overall is so acute that the UK government is now taking up vacancies in hotels nationwide (including some in the south-west) in order to house asylum-seeking refugees from abroad; yet local government is seemingly unable (unfunded?) to do likewise for the indigenous, homeless population *Note: the author is extremely sympathetic to the plight of refugees and commends those who mooted the idea, albeit the author concurs with the ultimate decision that cruise ships are unsuitable;*

2. Seemingly there are 3,800 people who are homeless in Devon and Cornwall including 1,500 children, according to **Shelter**. The fact that 1,500 children are homeless shames us all; it is a disgrace without parallel in the (relative affluence of the) twenty-first century. Quite

what the psychological impact is upon the mental health of such youngsters does not bear thinking about. The BBC found that the children suffered from tiredness, nightmares and bed-wetting.*

   * source: https://www.bbc.co.uk/news/uk-64889778

Despite the dreadful dilemma facing homeless people, Devon County Council announced as recently as March 2023 that it is withdrawing its £1.5 million p.a. grant to District councils within the county for homelessness (for rough sleepers and people in hostels), stating that it can no longer afford it. *

   *   source: https://www.northdevongazette.co.uk/plan-to-withdraw-1-5million-homelessness-fund-criticised-in-north-devon/

Both **West Devon** and **South Hams*** District Councils have declared a housing crisis. In part this is due to the number of people moving into the Districts since the COVID pandemic, buying houses and exacerbating the severely limited availability of homes for long-term rental. The second exacerbating factor is the number of second homes in Devon Districts, which is as follows:

   South Hams: 3,947
   East Devon: 2,687
   North Devon: 1,809
   Teignbridge: 1,320
   Torridge: 1,142
   Plymouth UA: 1,107
   West Devon: 650
   Exeter: 505
   Mid Devon: 196
   total   13,363

* As recently as December 2022, South Hams District Council announced plans to double council tax in 2024 for 4,000 second home owners (one property in twelve in the District is a second home). Torridge District Council has also voted for such a rise. *More on this later.*   source: https://www.bbc.co.uk/news/uk-england-devon-64040125

The number of homes available for rental nationwide has fallen by a third in the past eighteen months. This national trend might be expected to be even more acute in the desirable regions such as the South-west. The problem is getting worse, very substantially worse. As a consequence of reduced supply, rents have increased by 11% in the past 12 months. This is a burden falling on those sectors of society who are the most ill-placed to afford it. *

source: https://www.bbc.co.uk/news/business-65090846

The rising demand for houses and the inadequate supply of them, whether to live in, to buy-to-leave, to retain as second-homes or to be used for AirBnB, calls for a far-reaching and effective solution, one which will preserve a satisfactory number of affordable homes (for rental or purchase) for the incumbent people of Devon and Cornwall. This is long past desirable; it's now essential.

DaCSTaR is that solution.

The advent of AirBnB and social media promoting tourism has 'pulled the rug' on many families living in rented accommodation in popular tourist destinations, yet tourism has long been a mainstay of society and commerce in Devon and Cornwall; indeed, it is the biggest contributor to the economy of Cornwall.

It therefore seems somewhat absurd and paradoxical that the tourism driver of the economy is ripping away the homes from the relatively poorer people of the region, a great deal of whom serve that same tourism economy.

Of course, these difficulties have long been recognised by local government, but their efforts to resolve them have, largely thanks to severe financial constraints, been ineffective.

In Cornwall, it is estimated that the County Council loses council tax income of about £18 million p.a. because of second homes registered as businesses (but no Business Rates income is generated either as these will qualify for Small Business exemption).

Some Local Authorities see one solution as the imposition of a premium on Council Tax; indeed, so does the UK government, which now permits changes to the way second homes are taxed - i.e. a doubling of tax is allowed, but *for council tax purposes only*. However, this is likely to be counter-productive and self-defeating because the owner of the AirBnB property (faced with such a doubling) is perfectly entitled to switch their rental property (or that part of their home used for rental accommodation) to Business Rates; and, as they would (almost all of them) qualify for Small Business Rates Relief, they would not actually pay any Business Rates at all; in such circumstances neither would they pay any Council Tax! The result would be that the Local Authority actually loses Council Tax income completely but the property remains a tax-exempt (AirBnB) rental property.

Of course, the government has anticipated the probable switch to Business Rates - to some extent - with the necessity to offer and secure a minimum number of lettings; however, it is difficult to see how this can be monitored or, indeed, how fraudulent record-keeping in order to evade such mandatory requirements can even be detected.

Indeed, anyone who can afford a second home (and perhaps one not rented out to tourists) likely will be able to afford a premium Council Tax and so their property will remain unavailable for local housing.

In any event, the imposition of a premium Council Tax is exceedingly unlikely to lead to the creation (construction) of any more affordable homes in the significant numbers needed to resolve the scale of the problem (23,000 households on the waiting list in Cornwall, remember?), and hence the policy, ultimately and most likely, will be seen to be a failure.

Local government in the Counties and Districts professes an understanding of the economies of the two counties but devotes fairly miniscule resources to support the industries and commercial sectors of the economy.

However, to this author's mind, there seems to be only a limited ability to thoroughly connect and influence the 'linkages' between employment and housing in any way which would offer real and significant scope for very substantial and positive change. Perhaps that is the selfsame fruit of inadequate resources and, sadly, the acceptance of that fact by local authorities; indeed, it is surely a most reluctant conclusion to reach and doubtless a frustrating one for all concerned.

There is one particular aspiration within the 'northern Devon' tourism strategy / policy document (a joint paper from North Devon District and Torridge District councils) <u>which merits explicitly stating</u> within this introduction; it is one aspiration which wholly accords with the defined mechanisms and aspirations within *this* proposal:

"(the two councils will) explore with partners the scope and viability for sustainable transport solutions that add value for visitors and generate environmental and community benefits"

source:https://democracy.torridge.gov.uk/documents/s9168/Northern %20Devon%20Tourism%20Strategy%20FINAL.pdf (more on this later)

Meanwhile, the housing problem is gaining pace: Plymouth City reports a £37m budget 'hole'. The council blamed inflation, rising energy costs and increased demand for social care for the shortfall in its budget in 2023/2024.*

*source: https://www.bbc.co.uk/news/uk-england-devon-63552686

The growing lack of affordable housing throughout the peninsula will become an ever-increasing problem for local authorities, who are already struggling to find housing for evicted tenants; and in an era where the income for local authorities is also diminishing and their own financial position deteriorating, the catastrophe of evictions for people with nowhere to go will, unfortunately, accelerate.

A shocking headline of May 2022: **"Housing crisis is forcing locals to abandon their lives and leave Cornwall altogether."** A spokesperson for Cornwall County Council said: *"In a very small number of instances, we may have to offer accommodation outside Cornwall in the short term and as a last resort. We seek to move people back to Cornwall as soon as we can and continue to offer support to help them find long-term homes."* The term *"as soon as we can"* can hardly be much of a comfort for such persons affected who have lost their home, in probably the place where they grew up. **

** source https://www.cornwalllive.com/news/cornwall-news/housing-crisis-forcing-locals-abandon-7076661

Some enterprising young people, priced out of home ownership or even renting (who can afford the cost) are self-building low cost conversions of lorry trailers and portakabins or even living in motorhomes.*

*source:
https://www.theguardian.com/society/2023/jan/15/priced-out-uk-house-hunters-turn-to-lorry-sized-tiny-homes

Of course, much or most of this raises the question of planning permission or the absence of it, but it is a very visible barometer of desperation. It also raises the question of unsatisfactory water supply and sanitation (and the consequent prospects for pollution).

Recent UK tax changes have also compounded the problem of shortage of affordable rented accommodation in that landlords face higher taxes (mortgage costs cannot be deducted from letting income; instead, landlords can apply a 20% tax relief to mortgage payments, rather than the previous 40%). Furthermore, their difficulties are exacerbated by rising interest rates and increasing regulation. The latter might be considered as something of a mixed blessing if the intent to protect the tenant against poor maintenance, damp and mould also disincentivises the landlord from actually letting. Passing on all such cost increases are hard to justify (and sustain) to tenants. Sales of such properties will also face higher capital gains tax. *

* source: https://www.telegraph.co.uk/property/news/small-time-landlords-siege-bad-news-tenants/

The under-utilised hotels of the traditional tourist resorts of the region (including Torbay and Ilfracombe) and recently Exeter and Exmouth too are beginning, of late, to be populated by asylum-seekers; it is an increasing trend and one considered by Local Authorities as undesirable; indeed, several Councils are taking or looking to take legal action to block such eventualities.

However, it is another instance of **NOW** being the time to face uncomfortable facts: under-utilised-hotel owners need income, most particularly in the winter months. Assured income - from the Home Office - will certainly hold an appeal for hoteliers struggling with increased costs and staffing shortfalls.

For asylum-seekers, *it's better living in a lesser-grade hotel in Ilfracombe than in Albania.* Tens of thousands of young, male Albanians have made the perilous Channel crossing in 2022, an exponential rise on 2021, and more will continue to do so - the news has reached Albania: *"Come to the UK and stay in a hotel - there's no charge!"*

Seemingly, in March 2023, the government is now looking to end the practice of housing (at present) 51,000 people including asylum-seekers in (395) hotels, and is looking towards airbases and even (disused) ferries! *

* source: https://www.bbc.co.uk/news/uk-65074419

How many more asylum-seekers will come in 2023?

45,000 people crossed the Channel illegally in small boats in 2022. It certainly does not look like it is a problem that will go away in the short term or even at all. No flights have, as yet, taken off for Rwanda on the government's absurd scheme to reduce and disincentivise illegal immigration by flying them to far-distant Africa. *Note: the author has lived in equatorial Africa for a year (not in Rwanda) and it is not a place where principled people would send unfortunates to live.*

However, such is something of a diversion from the subject of this proposal: the solution to the housing crisis in Devon and Cornwall and the restoration of (rural) public transport in the form of restored railways.

How many more hotels will struggle or fail in the coming months?

How many of those same hotel owners will embrace salvation in the form of hosting asylum-seekers?

As a striking example of this, one hotel in Warwickshire which is a Grade II* Regency house set in 72 acres did welcome asylum-seekers in September 2021, to the extent of seeking to add 40 timber cabins within its grounds during 2022. This was embraced as salvation consequent to the Covid pandemic when tourist effectively ceased. The additional cabins embroiled the hotel and the local authority in a Planning dispute (*there's a surprise*). The locals, however, were refreshingly sympathetic to the asylum-seekers: *"everybody has got to live somewhere".* *

* source:
https://www.telegraph.co.uk/news/2022/11/12/migrant-hotel-breaches-planning-rules-glorified-sheds-house/

It seems incongruous to this author that the local authorities of Devon and Cornwall particularly cannot adopt a similar and embracing sympathy for indigenous local people who are homeless (and asylum-seekers too). It is, in fact, a tragedy which seems to be inadequately addressed and one which demands a far more radical approach to finding a solution.

DaCSTaR is that solution, as this document will try to show.

If Local Authorities wish to stymie a trend which they consider undesirable (and which will become increasingly inevitable as hoteliers face rising costs) then it is absolutely essential to offer an alternative to struggling hoteliers, a credible and viable one, one which will make a material difference. Currently, nothing of such ilk is even postulated, let alone offered.

DaCSTaR is that alternative, as this document will try to show.

Tinkering at the margins, as policymakers (both national and local) have long perpetuated, will increasingly be seen as futile; a 'joined up' solution is *urgently* needed, one which is more under the control of *local* communities and less subject to the whims of Whitehall and its present regime of cut taxes, cut spending, and ultimately cut quality of life for very many people in Devon and Cornwall.

Note: the author is *not* a proponent of state borrowing to solve all social ills; *the piper has, eventually, to be paid*; and it will be the future generations who will be blighted by UK state debt. It's perhaps true to say that we see the beginnings of that today: so-called Quantitative Easing (printing money) to facilitate the turning of the wheels of state in recent decades has, ultimately, brought the UK to the present position of increasing inflation and calls for cuts in spending and, concurrently, higher taxation.

The consequent devaluation of the pound makes imports more expensive, further stretching the budgets of everyone.

For all of the above reasons and problems including: the lack of public transport, the increasing struggle to preserve private car ownership, the deteriorating availability of affordable homes (both rented and owned), the deteriorating finances of public bodies, and the deteriorating economy generally, a more expansive and perhaps radical, but certainly innovative, set of solutions is called for.

Courageous minds, willing to accept and implement such exceptional measures, are also needed; yes, the old ways generally worked well and for a long time, but no more; the scale of the task is such that all inflexibilities in thinking must be discarded if progress on the requisite scale is to be achieved.

Panaceas are very hard to come by; national governments do not deliver them; and so this paper proposes that *local* government and communities within the South-West call upon *their own* resources - current and historical - to tackle the pressing needs of the peninsula, combining them into a solution which is within the reach of the existing, incumbent abilities of the peninsula, its people and its societal structures.

DaCSTaR is that solution.

The author commends it to the reader.

Alan Cartwright

This edition: April 2023

What is DaCSTaR?

DaCSTaR is: Devon and Cornwall Sustainable Travel and Regeneration

DaCSTaR is <u>not</u> an exercise in nostalgia; it is about the **future** <u>not the past</u>.

DaCSTaR is a viable path to prosperity for the region. The old maxim *"Where there's a will, there's a way"* has long been the philosophy of the author, and it seems wholly appropriate to the case.

DaCSTaR, in its fundamental mechanisms, opens a path to more and better affordable homes throughout the peninsula, both rented and owned; furthermore, it provides security of tenure within the tenancies which it can create, and it also lifts the financial burden from local authorities in doing so.

DaCSTaR is also therefore Devon and Cornwall Secure Tenant-assured Residencies

DaCSTaR defines an innovative application of the existing Section 106 Planning mechanism for Local Authorities to effectively raise local taxes, i.e. it does not increase either Council Tax, parking charges or any other existing local levies; neither does it call upon any central government financial resource or budget.

DaCSTaR is also therefore Devon and Cornwall Sustainable Taxation and Revenues

DaCSTaR is the opening of a door, a first glimpse of a potential future where the disparate towns, villages and even the smallest of rural settlements achieve a communication cohesion, one which is environmentally-friendly in view of the considerable potential for a diminution in car travel; indeed, it offers affordable transport for persons with no access to a private vehicle, and as such it opens up much easier access to travel for such persons all throughout Devon and Cornwall, and from further afield.

DaCSTaR offers a vision of a regional identity, a cohesion for the populace and society of the two south-west counties. It promotes a sense of community. It is an integration of policies: sufficient and sustainable housing with substantially enhanced and sustainable public transport.

DaCSTaR offers an alternative to road travel, both in part and in full for many journeys.

DaCSTaR offers the potential to put a hold, a pause at least, on expenditure on highways, and a similar halt to increasing traffic congestion.

DaCSTaR is the establishment of rail links to facilitate the economies of widespread and diverse population hubs by enabling mobility for the indigenous workforce and by attracting tourists in large numbers from within and without Devon and Cornwall; tourists who will spend significant, *substantial* sums within the two counties.

DaCSTaR defines a mechanism for restoring vastly improved rail links throughout Devon and Cornwall, including the 'lost' branch railway lines.

DaCSTaR is an idea, a concept, scarcely more than a preliminary to what, much more, will undoubtedly be required if the railway lines' restoration bud is ever to flower and the economic and societal ills of the South-West are to be comprehensively addressed.

DaCSTaR is also therefore Devon and Cornwall Sustainable Trains and Railways

Caveats: technical, research, financial

This document is aspirational but strictly limited in its detail; it is in no way definitive; it is intended to spark and thence develop interest and debate in its subject; it does not claim to be an authoritative document or proposal. It is an entirely amateur creation, one produced without the least funding and by an individual with no technical expertise whatsoever in the construction and maintenance of railways; as such, it is for others to identify the errors within and to develop the detail which is undoubtedly missing and which will be required if any elements of the **DaCSTaR** concept are developed into more substantive and detailed proposals for research funding, for any ultimate restoration of lost railway lines and for the creation of affordable homes.

The author of this preliminary-format or *conceptual* document is a lifelong entrepreneur; originally the founder-owner of a significant Midlands software development company and now a businessman living in the western part of Torridge District in northern Devon; a rural area which never had a railway (and which is never likely to have one).

Having stated that, the author has researched in great length the historical background to the present state of railways within *the northern regions of* Devon and Cornwall; indeed, there is a plethora of books with a great quantity of detail describing the lost railway lines, all readily available; it is fascinating reading (see the appendix).

Everything has its limits, and - *please note* - the **DaCSTaR** document is, *at this stage*, limited to those railways located or terminating in the *more northerly* regions of Devon and Cornwall, and including their route to Exeter and Plymouth; these are regions where rail transport has long been near wholly non-existent - except for just one line (the Tarka Line) linking Barnstaple to Exeter and a second line from Okehampton to Exeter (a line which was only relatively recently restored, in November 2021, after being closed for 49 years). Later editions will, ultimately, be extended to cover all other, omitted *'lost railways of Devon and Cornwall'*.

The peninsula, most particularly its rural regions, is an area which has a low population density and a consequently poor public transport provision. Despite this drawback, the author is minded that even the most remote rural areas such as this would much benefit from the restoration of railway lines as described within this document; this is because everyone bereft of a rail link could continue to travel either by car or even by bicycle to their nearest station (or halt) to gain the train and thereby complete the greater part of their journey on the train and not on the road.

This document avoids the technical terminology and marketing phraseology seemingly so beloved of many of the authors of specialised papers which are to be presented to an audience; indeed, with very few exceptions, the author has little knowledge of such, oft bewildering, vocabulary.

Doubtless there will be readers who will believe and perhaps even opine that this paper is simplistic, ill-conceived, unrealistic and the mere ramblings of a far-fetched imagination! Perhaps it really is; but that is to miss the point: the troubles and disadvantages under which the Devon and Cornwall peninsula has long laboured are growing; the housing shortage is a perpetual element in all local news media; the local authorities are reeling under an overload of debt and budget funding shortfalls, all at a time when the local population is rising to put a growing strain on their stretched resources; and there is no likelihood of increased funding coming from central government to assist local needs, none; and that is only likely to be exacerbated by central government cuts in all areas for the foreseeable few years and possibly longer. Nothing which is effective and which delivers a solution wholly adequate to the scale of the problem is happening.

Certainly, new homes are being built in significant quantities by the private sector in many parts of the peninsula; however, generally speaking, these houses will, naturally, sell for the open-market price that developers seek and expect; as such, many will be purchased by incomers to the region but relatively few will be 'affordable homes'.

Neither will there likely be any mechanism to preserve the *status quo* of any such affordable homes. Furthermore, none are being built to be long-term *rental* properties and neither are any of them being made available by developers to Local Authorities for the housing of homeless people; these underlying problems are simply not being addressed on the necessary scale.

Local authorities are participating in affordable home projects; Torridge District Council, for example, to its great credit is involved with the creation of a little over fifty in Great Torrington; but Torridge is a big place, there are many other locations which also need affordable housing, and at the present rate it is unlikely to happen in the lifetimes of those struggling to find or keep a roof over their heads; there is no funding available on the requisite scale: that is incontrovertible.

Something imaginative, something creative, something radical, is now necessary, and quite possibly has been so for a considerable time. The needs of the peninsula are increasingly acute; as such, they are akin to, on a smaller scale, the accepted necessity to address climate change. Fortunately, in this case, it is only the people of Devon and Cornwall - and their elected representatives - who have to be convinced; and - *we can be grateful* - that is perfectly possible if local government, the press, influencers generally and the widespread population all put their shoulders to the task.

A better future, an end to the affordable homes crisis, and a greater prosperity *is* achievable; and it is so *within our foreseeable lifetime*. Every reader is urged to seize the opportunity *and to act* in any and every way within their own capabilities to resolve the crisis.

Alan Cartwright

March 2023

*Postscript: The author would like to thank **Bernard Mills** for enthusiastically responding to the call for suitable photographs with which the author has better illustrated many points within this document.*

What is the fundamental mechanism to achieve the stated objectives?

The national economy, at the time of writing in November 2022, is heading for what (it has been reported) might likely be the longest recession for a hundred years. It is a simplistic statement and does not refer to the *depth* of the recession, the *extent* of the economic downturn.

The recession will bear down most hard upon the poorest members of society; ageing cars will be perpetuated and 'old bangers' will remain longer on the road; energy has become much more expensive, even verging on near-wholly unaffordable for the poorest in society; rented accommodation - already rare - will diminish further or deteriorate in standard as landlords quit and repairs become unaffordable (the price of building materials and contractors has soared in the past twelve months); tourism will decline and accommodation providers in such as hotels will opt for (in effect) assured income from state-subsidised guests such as asylum-seekers (it's already happening in Ilfracombe); ultimately, all of these factors will also create an increase in crime as (some) increasingly desperate people reach the end of their already slim resources but have to find a means to enable them to eat, to stay warm and dry.

Alarming stuff!

Yes, but the south-west region has long been at the lower end of the national scale on many measures: income per capita, housing, transport *etc*. For these hugely-important reasons, it is surely time that influencers, policy-makers within and without the region, local government and every organisation contemplate a more innovative, even radical, method to reverse the trend, to aid the poorest of society, to resolve the regional housing shortage and to regenerate the regional economy.

Pie in the sky?

No, not really; it can be done. It will require the broad acceptance of a new approach, a target which all in the region can visualise and aspire to; more than aspire, to reach for. The longest and deepest recession of a hundred years ago began in the USA in 1929 after the

Wall Street Crash and endured until 1933; in terms of *depth*: 17% of farm loans were foreclosed on, manufacturing output fell by a third and prices fell by 20%; indeed, it was called the Great Contraction, popularly known as The Depression.

In the United States, one man with a radical approach was elected President on the back of a (for the times) radical proposal; it was called "**The New Deal**"; it promised relief for the unemployed and for the poor, and recovery of the economy back to normal levels. The President was Franklin D. Roosevelt. A Democrat beat the incumbent Republican candidate (Herbert Hoover) by a voters' landslide because people had had enough and wanted change: they wanted a very big change for the better. That is what the south-west region has long required and, *importantly*, it can be done: **DaCSTaR** could be the driver of "**The New Deal**" for the region.

One of the targets of **The New Deal** was stimulation of the private house-building sector. That, for the northern regions of Devon and Cornwall is the true "low-hanging fruit", the resource or mechanism with which to regenerate the regional economy, if - that is - it is embraced by local government and the region's populace more generally. The important thing is: it is genuinely within reach; it can enable so much that will be beneficial for the region, for its population, its housing, its commerce and its transport services, particularly rail - *the subject of this paper.*

In relatively recent years there has been a degree of debate about the potential restoration of lost railway lines; indeed, those linking Tavistock to Bere Alston and (to a lesser degree) Tavistock to Okehampton have seen tentative first steps, but nothing of them has yet happened (at the time of writing); and that does not bode well for the considerably greater potential within the region for more lines to be restored to serve more widespread communities in a sustainable way, a way that could be economically and socially very advantageous to the towns, villages, businesses and people of this region.

The councils of the region, including the County Councils and the District authorities all produce documentation on Tourism and its contribution to the local economies; such reports usually suggest strategies to encourage tourism; for example, the 'northern Devon' document (of Torridge and North Devon District councils combined) advocates:

> *"developing the tourism business",*
>
> *"engaging with visitors",*
>
> *"developing capacity",*
>
> *"working positively to deliver joined-up solutions",*
>
> *"new business opportunities and productivity gains",*
>
> *"preferring 'wise-growth'",*
>
> *"developing and delivering social benefits",*
>
> *"working with key partners",*
>
> *"supporting the Biosphere Reserve",*
>
> *"supporting the Coastal Community Teams",*
>
> *"developing action plans",*
>
> *"working with transport operators to enhance the visitor journey", etc.*

One might be forgiven for wondering to what extent all of this laudable aspiration, so polished in its presentation, will result in tangible, meaningful, significant and substantial benefits to the local populace.

It also raises a deal of questions:

Is there any substance to it?

Will it result in a boost to affordable housing?

Will it create one extra mile of railway? Or even one extra bus?

Will it bring a significant number of additional tourists to the region? If so, how?

And, were it to do so, where will they stay?

Will more local people be evicted from their homes in order to accommodate these extra tourists in AirBnB's?

Critically, do any of the local authorities actually state where they will find the necessary substantial funds (millions would be needed to make an effective difference) to deliver their stated objectives?

No, they do not; because, simply stated, such funds on the requisite, significant scale, unfortunately, do not exist. The document is essentially an aspiration; but, sadly, it is little more than a fiction, one born of laudable sentiment. The more cynical mind might even consider it to be a fable projected for public consumption.

Far from the stated objective of a "joined up" strategy, these statements are disparate and entirely lacking in mechanism.

Where is the explanation of the mechanism to actually deliver the resources which would be required to deliver the stated objectives?

Therein is the reality: there isn't a strategy; certainly not one that is sufficiently defined with appropriate mechanisms, one able to be implemented with sufficient resources: <u>there are no resources</u>. Sad to say, it seems to be an exercise in futility.

[NB The reader is asked to note that the author has no wish to denigrate the commendable efforts and aspirations of local authorities.]

At least there is *one* stated aspiration within this 'northern Devon' policy document which accords with the defined mechanisms and aspirations within *this, the author's* proposal: *"explore with partners the scope and viability for sustainable transport solutions that add value for visitors and generate environmental and community benefits"*

Well, Torridge and North Devon District Councillors (and others too), please note: here is the *sustainable transport **solution*** which *adds value for visitors*; indeed, DaCSTaR is one that encourages <u>more</u> visitors; it *generates environmental benefits* with a diminution in road travel, and it *benefits the community by virtue of resolving the affordable homes (both rented and owned) crisis.* Here is the substance, the tool, with which to implement the identified and desirable objectives of the "northern Devon" plan: *please read on.*

The following lines are sourced from Wikipedia:

- "**Tourism** is the biggest contributor to the Cornish economy. For Devon it is also hugely significant.
- **Mining** for tin and copper was carried on in Devon from ancient times until the 1930s.
- Since the rise of seaside resorts with the arrival of the railways in the 19th century, Devon's economy has been heavily reliant on tourism. The county's economy has followed the declining trend of British seaside resorts since the mid-20th century,
- Like neighbouring <u>Cornwall</u> to the west, <u>Devon</u> is disadvantaged economically compared to other parts of southern England, owing to the decline of a number of core industries, notably **fishing, mining and farming**.
- Approximately 80% of land in the South West of England is in **agricultural** use."

Local authority conceptual strategies are at least correct in identifying **Tourism** as the sector which should be encouraged. **Mining** is unlikely to return; lithium mining in Cornwall has been mentioned, as has tungsten mining near Plymouth; but those alone are incapable of generating *widespread* societal benefits. **Fishing** is under sustained attack from over-fishing, from foreign fleets and from the effective closure of markets consequent to the more detrimental results of BREXIT; indeed, *"the governor of the Bank of England, the Office for Budget Responsibility (OBR) and the Organisation for Economic Co-operation and Development (OECD) all agree that, notwithstanding Covid or the Ukrainian war, Brexit is the main reason why **the UK is the only economy in the G7 still below its pre-pandemic size**"**; and on that point I will add no more as we would find ourselves wandering towards politics, which is the end of all comfortable talk.

*source: The Guardian
https://www.theguardian.com/commentisfree/2022/dec/11/signs-are-clear-our-destiny-lies-with-europe-not-sovereign-global-britain-fantasy

Agriculture and its consequent river pollution is increasingly under scrutiny, its economic viabilty under threat and its workforce ageing. The author's farmer neighbour stated this summer that it was not viable to crop the author's fields of long grass for hay because of the price of (untaxed, red) diesel fuel!

The threats to the South-West rural economy have never been greater. A radical approach to find one or more effective solutions is increasingly essential.

DaCSTaR is that solution.

Devon and Cornwall are desirable locations for tourism; it is a statement which has endured for a hundred years even as the transport to reach the peninsula has varied and the accommodation too in more recent years has experienced great flux in style and substance. Indeed, tourism supports 1 in 5 jobs in Cornwall. Tourism, therefore, must be promoted; yet, this must not be so with the undesirable consequence being the noted loss of homes for the people of the peninsula. This is a proven problem requiring of a solution.

It must be borne in mind that Tourism is *not* a hugely profitable sector (the author has worked in the industry for 30 years, in accommodation particularly). Two question arise, therefore:

How are additional tourists to be attracted to Devon and Cornwall?

If rental tenants are not to be evicted to make way for AirBnB tourists, where is any additional tourist accommodation to come from and how is it to be funded?

Promotional bodies for both Devon and Cornwall have strived for years and with a degree of success to boost tourism, but it might be thought that their offer has crystallised to simply a repetition of the well known natural resources of beaches plus generic messages about accommodation. The UK population is long aware of all that, but they aren't fooled; they go to foreign parts for assured better weather. There is absolutely nothing that any promotional message originating from any organisation in the South-West will do to change that. To believe and act otherwise is to condemn the South-West to no change.

Hence, the most fundamental prerequisite to resolve is: **what will bring more tourists to the region?**

Iconic attractions such as Tim Smit's Eden Project doubtless attract tourists in huge numbers and as part of a Cornwall holiday. Rick Stein's fish restaurants undoubtedly have had a huge and positive impact for Padstow; St. Ives, the town, long a venue for art, is similarly successful. All of these provide an essential pointer, a clue: <u>Provide something</u> **which is exceptional in character** <u>and/or quality, and people will seek it out</u>, will travel, will pay, will stay, will generate tourism-related employment.

Ultimately, these exceptional projects do bring tourists, <u>but they do not fund affordable homes</u>. Neither are there enough of them, and they are discretely-located, i.e. they are in *specific* places.

Many hundreds of thousands of tourists flock to Devon and Cornwall throughout the spring, summer and autumn, almost all of them arriving *by car*.

A *more widespread* appeal, a distribution of a unique attraction, is needed to generate the massive increase in volume and value that the South-West needs to achieve a *widespread* regeneration, *an endemic renaissance*, and one which is to the benefit of all living here.

Imagine the appeal of a 'Grand Tour' *by rail* on a restored network of rural branch lines throughout the scenic splendour of the Devon and Cornwall countryside, a tour which could be enjoyed from the unhurried train window, before patronising the many and varied restaurants, hotels and guest houses of the peninsula overnight. This is the *widespread* appeal of an attraction which by its very nature would be created (restored) all throughout the peninsula.

DaCSTaR is that solution.

The smallest of trains (standard gauge that is), a single carriage "Diesel Multiple Unit or DMU". The perfect train for commuting into the region's towns from its villages and hamlets. Perfect, that is, until it becomes feasible in future to provide electrification.

Photo: Bernard Mills.

It is no surprise to suggest that anything big, big in investment, big in appeal, big in value *etc* **mandates substantial capital investment**; however, as the author understands very well, the commercial margins for the varied segments of the tourism sector are not large; indeed, they are such that they cannot compete with innovative uses for resources in other sectors *which will consume such capital as may be available.* It seems an insoluble problem, a tough nut to crack; *and it is.*

DaCSTaR is the solution.

Devon and Cornwall have one extremely effective asset, almost wholly untapped, undeveloped, unexploited: people in other regions of the UK have a great affinity for the two counties, so much so that there is a perpetual demand for houses *from incomers.* This also acts to the detriment of local Devonians and Cornish people who can find themselves effectively 'priced out' of the housing market, putting more pressure on a shrinking rental housing stock and ultimately burdening the local authorities with an insuperable financial problem to accommodate homeless people.

DaCSTaR is the solution.

The total population of *rural* Devon County - excluding the three unitary authorities of Exeter, Torbay and Plymouth (within which another half-million people live) is illustrated below:

1981	599,200	population growth
1991	658,500	+10% over a decade
2001	705,600	+7% over a decade
2011	747,709	+13.5% over a decade
2021	810,716	+8.4% over a decade
and		
2022	827,659	+2% year on year

This is a 38% increase in population since 1981; i.e. over 41 years it is an annualised increase of, broadly, 1% per annum. **A lot** of people are moving to Devon (and Cornwall), and that trend should be utilised *for the benefit of all the populace* rather than the minority who are developers. Local authorities have the powers to achieve that.

Devon's land area is 2,534 square miles (including the relatively smaller areas of the unitary authorities). The Devon County population density is therefore 326 persons per square mile, or (at an average 2.31 residents per household) 141 homes per sq. mile. Of course, the majority of homes are within the relatively urban towns and villages, and the rural landscape has a much lower density of housing; and that is perpetuated by the Planning Policy predilection against permitting new rural dwellings.

However, whilst the <u>National Planning Policy precludes rural houses being built</u> because of pressure on poor rural roads (and there is no budget to improve those), there is perhaps a worthwhile exception to be explored or created: houses with immediate access to a railway.

But there are no (well, very few) rural railways!

If the former (fairly comprehensive) network of branch railway lines were to be restored, it is fair to say and expect that *at least* some *small* degree of pressure on roads would diminish. To what extent is impossible to project with any degree of confidence; however, it might seem *not unreasonable* to believe that road travel by the whole (or at least the majority) of Devon's 1.3 million population on rural roads might diminish *slightly*; and were *slightly* to even marginally exceed the additional road traffic generation from that additional housing which would be permitted and built in close proximity to railway access, then it might be an acceptable trade-off in order to gain a *significant* increase in housing stock, specifically too in *affordable* housing stock.

But how does that new housing stock benefit such folk who have no access to affordable homes?

DaCSTaR is the solution.

New homes in the relatively rural environments of Devon County and Cornwall will always attract a premium price (both relative and absolute). In rural Torridge where the author lives it is difficult to find the most modest (and ageing) bungalow for sale at a price much less than £400,000. A *new* open-market house would easily sell for, say, £430,000, particularly so when located in a relatively rural location.

Such a building would cost (broadly stated) about £125,000 to build from new *(materials have increased in price very substantially throughout 2022)*. Allowing £5,000 for the house (land) plot *(see more below on how that low figure is attained)*, £10,000 for services and road access, and £20,000 for builder's profit, a total £160,000 is expended.

[Note: the author has built 65 (predominantly) three-bedroom (holiday) homes over the past 22 years, and so has some degree of building experience.]

Assuming a new home selling price of £400,000 and £160,000 of costs as above, the premium (net of all costs) is (broadly stated) £240,000. Of this net sum:

(i) were £110,000 to go into a fund for railway restoration, and
(ii) £150,000 were to go into a fund for building **affordable** homes for local people *(the affordable homes might be slightly smaller in construction size and hence slightly cheaper to build, say £115,000; plus £5,000 for the land, £10,000 for services and road access, and £20,000 builder's profit, total cost per affordable home being £150,000)*, then
(iii) £10,000 would remain to provide a contribution to diverse social care costs within the Districts.

To reiterate, the greatly beneficial outcome is:

(a) 10,000 open-market homes are built *in close proximity to a restored railway* (station or rural halt), and sold to incomers to the region, each of whom will be paying £430,000; of which, £270,000 goes to the public purse;

and

(b) 10,000 new affordable homes are also built; 50% of which might be sold (with suitable covenants to maintain the status as affordable - *more on that below**) and 50% of which could be rented *or* used by the local authority to accommodate such persons as they deem desirable and requiring of accommodation;

and

(c) 10,000 worthwhile cash contributions are generated, each of £10,000 (**a cumulative £100 million**), to assist the social care costs of participating local authorities' expenditure.

* an affordable home, bought for (say) the £150,000 original build cost price, *when sold on the open market* by the first and successive owners sees a proportion of the sale price retained by the seller (calculated as the build cost or the cost price plus a suitable index of house-price inflation) and the remainder would be retained by the local authority (or such other suitable organisation such as a charitable trust - *more on this below*) within a specific fund for (further) affordable house building.

A suitable covenant would be included in the initial sale Transfer, and there is also legislation to enforce this within the Housing and Planning Act 2016, Chapter One, Paragraph 3:

> (1)The restrictions on sale that may be specified... in relation to a dwelling that has been sold to a qualifying first-time buyer include, in particular, restrictions:
>
> (a) requiring a person who sells the dwelling within a specified period to make a payment to a specified person in respect of the starter homes discount, or
>
> (b) prohibiting a person from selling the dwelling within a specified period unless the dwelling is sold to a qualifying first-time buyer at a discount.

Note that the affordable homes might likely be *a mixture* of single-bedroom, two-bedroom, three-bedroom and four-bedroom homes, such that County and District Councils can allocate a suitable home to those in need of one; as such, *more* than 10,000 affordable homes might well be created within the budget available.

The affordable homes would all be to a standard design, such that a myriad local builders constructing them would impose a minimalist call upon the architects and owners (a Charitable Trust) during tendering and construction. Building design changes and the associated administrative burden of such would not be entertained.

To return to the restoration of the 'lost' railways: to the sceptical mind; indeed, to the mind long accustomed to the almost complete absence of branch railway lines in Devon and Cornwall, the suggestion that such lines could (a) actually *be* restored (b) be financially viable and (c) could deliver worthwhile and significant benefits might seem incredible, perhaps even wholly without the least basis in fact; however, that is not the case, as this paper will seek to explain.

A few remaining branch railway lines do still exist, lines which deliver meaningful benefits in terms of reducing car traffic, reducing pollution, reducing road congestion, and delivering a more satisfactory mode of travel for the commuter.

After sixty years, the time is ripe to re-evaluate the potential for the 'lost' lines and their potential future benefits to society in Devon and Cornwall in the twenty-first century.

DaCSTaR endeavours to do that.

Why is a railway restoration an essential element of this scheme?

This is a particularly relevant question in the light of two crucial (*but most usually disconnected in thinking*) elements of today's society: **housing** and **transport**; indeed, it is crucial that a satisfactory, credible answer is explained, understood and accepted before serious consideration can possibly be given to what, superficially, appears to be no more than a flight of fantasy.

The desperate state of public and affordable private housing has already been described, and so the author will turn to the transport element of this question.

As a society we aspire, in the interests of the environment generally, to reduce road traffic; but in the regions the subject of this proposal, public transport is positively skeletal for almost everywhere in rural areas. Indeed, the few bus services are struggling and will not survive without subsidy.

Bidding for £1.4 bn of state funds for improving bus services for the *three* years 2021, 2022 and 2023 resulted in only 25% of local authorities receiving any money (applications exceeded £9 bn). *

** source:
https://www.theguardian.com/politics/2022/jan/23/boris-johnsons-bus-back-better-red-wall-levelling-up-treasury-cuts-funding*

That bus services for rural areas are inadequate hardly requires further explanation, but where else will the money come from for enhancements? The Council Tax payer who is facing the present hardships of increases in such, as well as inflation generally, is not likely to welcome paying more, particularly so for a service which, in most cases, he /she is unlikely to use. And, it must be asked, would rural dwellers go to the supermarkets, for example, (which are located within towns) by bus? Unlikely. Hence, it must be asked: how can this fundamental incongruity be resolved?

The answer must be: build new homes adjacent to or very near to restored railway (lines) stations and halts, i.e. make it easy to travel from those same stations to those towns where the supermarkets exist.

However, there are fundamental blocks to such an approach. Setting aside for the moment the issue of funding railway restoration, the National Planning Policy - for the most part - precludes building homes (*or anything else*) in rural areas; the countryside has, seemingly, been abandoned by the state! To the author's mind this seems to be a dreadful and fundamental error. Yes, the reasons are understood and have a degree of validity: the rural roads are in an absolutely dire state, akin to Third World standards with so many potholes (*enough said on this aspect*); there is effectively a hopelessly inadequate public transport system and no funds to improve it; and rural travel in almost every respect, certainly by car, has been blighted by the concerns for further environmental degradation.

But it cannot possibly be right to write off rural Devon and Cornwall, to condemn it to being the preserve of only the farmer and the rich. That is not what Devon and Cornwall fundamentally are. Many rural areas elsewhere in Europe are proactively struggling *against* rural depopulation; whole villages exist in rural Spain and Italy, for example, where the population has dwindled to only the oldest persons, leaving the most ghastly legacy of total inactivity and the absence of all social cohesion and facilities. That is an extreme example, admittedly; however, the small and rural villages and settlements of Devon and Cornwall desperately need investment, housing, public transport connectivity and a community cohesion with neighbouring towns and also access to the more major cities.

The first ingredient, therefore, is a fundamental re-evaluation of where we see the future for rural populations: do we wish to see rural depopulation or thriving communities within widespread villages, hamlets and (important this) a public transport hub for scattered rural homes? The thinking of beauracracy must change; that is the first essential.

A comprehensive network of restored railways will serve several purposes:

(i)   It will be the tool or justification for:

(a)   deviating from the National Planning Policy Framework (NPPF) and granting planning permission for the building of the <u>rural</u>

housing stock *with premium pricing* which is the underlying, fundamental source of finance for the comprehensive economic and housing regeneration of the whole region of Devon and Cornwall; and

(b)   the acquisition via purchase or (less likely) compulsory appropriation for the rural land which is required for housing *(as well as railways)* at no more than double the agricultural value (i.e. such land would cost far more within or close to the boundaries of established settlements - *more on this later*; and

(c)   it provides for the new homes approved and built to be accessible without imposing an additional road traffic burden on rural roads (when considered 'in the round' i.e. with the reduction of road traffic *more generally* by virtue of <u>the wider population also making use of the new railways</u> for certain aspects of travel (and in doing so replacing the use of their cars); indeed, *it has the potential to diminish road traffic generally throughout the whole peninsula;*

(ii)   the existing i.e. the *incumbent* population would use the railway to commute to and from work; for example: live in Ilfracombe and commute to work in Barnstaple. This accords with the stated local policy objective;

(iii)   the existing i.e. the *incumbent* population will use the railway to gain access to the *mainline* railway at places where, at present, they have to drive quite some distance in order to park and access a train (Tiverton Parkway has a huge catchment area);

(iv)   incoming tourists will once again use the railway to reach the historically traditional tourist resorts such as Ilfracombe and Bude;

(v)   it would be feasible to operate the hugely-appealing "steam train specials", and 'train' tourists would be attracted to the region (such is much less likely with diesel commuter trains). Such "steamers" would ideally operate on a well-publicised and frequent timetable, running daily and working between a number of towns and destinations, attracting tourists in very substantial numbers: a 'Mecca' for enthusiasts. **This would be the *'widely-distributed'* equivalent of such as the Eden Project, except that the benefits go to a *widely-distributed* number of accommodation providers throughout the region, particularly so in those towns such as Ilfracombe which are slipping into decay.**

(vi)   Restoration of lost railway lines will mean - *in those areas the subject of this paper* - very substantial investment:

(i) 20,000 houses / £3.1 **billion** invested in housing stock,

(ii) 250 miles of railway lines restored (broadly stated, a £1 **billion** budget - *see later in this document*),

(iii) a sum of about £150-200 million in trains and rolling stock, plus station and halt construction (including land appropriation);

(iv) about £100 million contributed to social care;

a total of in excess of £4.3 billion pounds of investment in the region and a golden age for all construction enterprises.

For these reasons, **DaCSTaR** is also therefore:

Devon and Cornwall Sustainable Trains and Railways

Is this the time to contemplate such an investment when the UK economy is facing difficult challenges?

As much as times were swiftly changing in the 1950s and 1960s, when wealth distribution was rising and the majority of the populace had access to a car (shunning the inconvenience of the train), the present times also indicate that significant and substantial changes are coming; indeed, the harbingers of change are plainly visible:

1. Putin's war has plunged western Europe into an intense period of reflection on energy, its sources and uses;

2. COVID and its consequent approach to working from home has so substantially diminished the workforce (as people opt not to go back) that there is no longer any significant unemployment: many people have wholly given up working, older folk more particularly;

3. There is a shortage of labour generally, consequent to the above, and this militates against people working in the tourism sector, which is not well-paid in comparison to a broad range of other employment opportunities;

4. The catastrophic dabbling of Truss and Kwarteng in the UK fiscal budget and (tax and spend) mechanisms of state has succeeded in bringing an end to the long-held illusion that the state can continue to borrow indefinitely to meet its outgoings; and as a result the emphasis (which may last only until the next general election) of the present government is on reducing public expenditure and increasing taxation to decrease the fiscal deficit. One (so far rejected) potential consequence of this may yet be the (eventual) scrapping of HS2 (£156bn cost projected);

5. BREXIT, that triumph of self-promotion for Boris and his Little Englanders, has failed; only the most subjective and blinkered of minds can now doubt that. BREXIT has blighted the UK in its relationship with the EU countries, blighted the stability of the Irish *status quo* - i.e. the near-miraculous accommodation between extremes - and blighted the transit of many UK exports, food particularly, to the extent that, for example, the trade in shellfish has

collapsed (a hit to the Cornish economy); only today (21st Nov. 2022) it has been announced that an Icelandic fish-processing firm is pulling out of Grimsby because of BREXIT, and 400 UK jobs there have been lost; *source: the Guardian*

https://www.theguardian.com/business/2022/nov/21/200-jobs-at-risk-as-icelandic-fish-processing-firm-pulls-out-of-uk-brexit-coronavirus

6.   The consequence of much, perhaps all, of the above is (a) a diminution of what government (both central and local) will be able to afford in order to fund affordable housing and (b) a fast-surging rise in UK inflation, which will erode the value of people's savings, and in doing so diminishing their propensity to spend (including on tourism).

This 'perfect storm', this combination of powerful and generally negative impacts on people and their income, already demonstrates greater pressure on household budgets; the postponing of car repairs & maintenance is just one example.

Innovative solutions are required; *plodding along* with the self-delusion that *"everything will be all right"* is not going to work; indeed, that day of fundamental realisation is fast approaching for even the most sceptical.

Retail industries are increasingly in the firing line, as a BBC report on 9th November illustrates:

"Marks and Spencer has warned of a "gathering storm" of higher costs for retailers and pressure on household budgets as it reported a fall in profits for the first half of the year.

The High Street giant said trading would become "more challenging" after it revealed its profits dropped by **24%.**

It said "all parts" of retail would be affected by the UK's economic climate; adding, **unviable firms would go bust**.

But M&S said its business could "prove more resilient" due to its clientele.

Many UK businesses are being hit by rising energy bills, wage costs and raw materials prices.

Consumers are also cutting back their spending, with the Bank of England warning the UK is facing its longest recession since records began.

M&S said the "combined impacts of the cost-of-living squeeze" and the increased cost of doing business was "creating pressure on margins industry-wide".

source: https://www.bbc.co.uk/news/business-63566945

Now more than ever, the south-west peninsula needs a vision for change, backed by a plan **of substance** to deliver that change. The scale of the economic and housing challenge is of such a magnitude that what is needed is a strategy on the scale of a **NEW DEAL**; it is hard to conclude otherwise without indulging in indifference or reckless optimism; the time is now, nothing less will really do.

DaCSTaR is that solution:

1. it can resolve many of the ills that beset the tourism sector; and
2. it is a resolution of the shortage of affordable accommodation throughout the region and a mechanism to house the homeless; and
3. it is a strategy with which to boost economic growth in the peninsula generally and to a significant extent - and to do so **with powers and resources that do not require UK central government state aid or investment in a time of national crisis. The solution is here, locally, within Devon and Cornwall.**

But how could a modern-day railway succeed when Dr Beeching closed lines which were extremely unprofitable?

In brief, there are a number of helpful factors which did not exist in the 1960s at the time of the branch line closures; these include:

• The historic railway was labour-intensive, a great number of staff were engaged at every point of the network. That huge number would have to be greatly reduced:

A guard often attended rural level crossings. Such can be automated with modern technology. No gates would be necessary, only traffic lights. Photo: Bernard Mills.

DaCSTaR ®   Devon and Cornwall Sustainable Travel and Regeneration   38

• the design and creation of a public body (perhaps established as a charitable trust - *more on that later*) which can own and control a restored railway network, <u>and which is not burdened by the least debt</u>;

• an assured income flow which will always be greater than the possibility of any incurred *operating* losses of such a network (more home creation can be added into the same programme if required);

• a community-wide and held close participation in control and involvement in management of the restored network, augmented by the very real participation of (low or nil cost) local volunteers;

• a proven tourism appeal with steam trains running widely on a restored network on a frequent and regular, timetabled basis.

The following pages explore these factors in greater detail.

The proposal to restore lost railways is not unique; railway lines **are** being restored in the UK; **The "Great Central" heritage railway is one such.** It is a currently-ongoing project which aims to reunify 18 miles of railway line (broadly equivalent to the Barnstaple to Ilfracombe line, for example). It will replace an ageing bridge over the road below it, and - *significantly* - its principal objective is to offer a *heritage railway experience* to its users:

source: https://www.therailwayhub.co.uk/64830/bridge-demolition-puts-railway-project-on-track/

The lost railways: What happened?

To begin to shape a grasp of the future it is sensible to begin by looking *back*, to learn and understand from the past. Our lives in the twenty-first century are what we understand very well, and the era of even a hundred and fifty years ago - *with all of the limitations in everyday life of such times* - seems so remote as to be almost incomprehensible; indeed, in today's era of the photograph, the television, the phone in hand (a phone which is far more powerful than the small computers of even ten years ago), the known, understood and memorable element of the past for many of us oft seems to stretch back only as far as our childhood.

Hence, social changes of the *nineteenth* century are little-known or recognised by the average man (and probably are of little interest too); indeed, the camera and photograph (which increasingly epitomise "the news") only emerged in the latter half of the 19th century.

What is apparent with even the sketchiest of historical research is the lack of any transport until the mid-19th century other than the horse (and carriage, average speed 8 mph and expensive for the 'ordinary' man; indeed, when the first motor omnibus entered service, the police interfered because it travelled faster than 8 mph).

Hence, the emergence of the train was - to everyone - something of a marvel; a steam engine was a leading-edge development, and it offered for the first time the prospect of comfortable and longer-distance travel, even if it was limited to the more affluent in the early years. However, investor interest rapidly developed which lead to the emergence of railway lines and a vast network which ultimately overlaid most of the country (England at least, Scotland and Wales to a lesser extent) and linked every population centre together and facilitated travel for the common man, for the working class; for the first time introducing the concept of a (annual) holiday to every household, however poor. The line to Ilfracombe (which will be used as an example in much of this document) opened in 1874.

The UK rail network at its peak began in earnest in the mid-nineteenth century and very rapidly swept over all the well-populated regions of the UK with scores, indeed hundreds, of branch lines.

Railway expansion at this time was rapid: between 1826 and 1836 378 miles of track had opened. By the time the South Eastern Railway opened as far as Dover in 1844, 2,210 miles of line had been opened, making travel around the country faster, more comfortable and less expensive. *

Railways allowed people to travel further and more quickly. This allowed leisure travel and contributed to the growth of seaside resorts. It also allowed people to live further from their places of work as the phenomenon of commuting took hold. *

*source: https://www.parliament.uk/about/living-heritage/transformingsociety/transportcomms/roadsrail/kent-case-study/introduction/railways-in-early-nineteenth-century-britain/

By 1870 Britain had about 13,500 miles (21,700 km) of railway. At the system's greatest extent, in 1914, there were about 20,000 miles (32,000 km) of track, **run by 120 competing companies** (astonishing to the modern mind). The British government combined all these companies into four main groups in 1923 as an economy measure.
source: https://www.britannica.com/topic/British-Railways

For an early history (which is outside the scope of this document), read: *https://www.campop.geog.cam.ac.uk/research/projects/transport/onlineatlas/railways.pdf*

One simple illustration / example of the popularity of such railway lines to coastal south-west towns is the number of trains and tourists that would travel on a peak summer Saturday to the Victorian-era resort of Ilfracombe: **ten thousand** tourists would arrive by train (25 trains in all) on a single day in the 1950s! Such a number is scarcely imaginable today. Yet it was but a few more years, 1970, when the line closed, after a lifespan of just 96 years.

Two factors were influential in the demise: the coming of the car and the recession (the depression) of the early 1930s. Here are a few statistics: the first of which illustrates the negative effect of the recession:

1. Tickets *issued* at Ilfracombe in **1928**: 213,763 and in **1936**: 112,751, down 47%
2. Tickets *collected* at Ilfracombe in **1928**: 407,137 and in **1936**: 236,611, down 42%

Then came the war in 1939, when all railways would have been perceived as vital to the wartime economy; any deliberations about changes or economy measures were postponed.

World War Two effectively bankrupted Great Britain, which resulted in John Maynard Keynes orchestrating a loan from the USA in the sum of $3.75 billion at 2% interest for 50 years.

Little known to today's public is that many of the 19th century railway lines never made a penny piece of profit for their promoters, ultimately resulting in the swallowing up of all of them by the big four railway companies: Great Western Railway (GWR), Southern Railway (SR), London Midland and Scottish (LMS) and the London and North-Eastern Railway (LNER). Even so, the plain economics dictated by the operational costs of the vast branch network proved too much to sustain, even for the four behemoths; and in 1948 all were taken over by the state, nationalised.

However, as the UK entered the 1950s, personal lifestyles improved, to the point where Harold Macmillan famously declared that *"the people had never had it so good"*. This was certainly reflected in car ownership, a huge trend which was overtaking British life. For the first time "the man in the street" could afford a car. The percentage of households <u>owning a car</u> was:

1950	**1960**	1970	1980	1990	2000	2010
17%	35%	50%	60%	66%	72%	75%
trend	**+106%**	+43%	+20%	+10%	+9%	+4%

The resultant decline in the <u>number of trains arriving</u> on peak season Saturdays at Ilfracombe (for example) is illustrated as follows:

Year	1909	1925	1932	1958	**1964**
trains:	17	19	24	25	18
	trend	+12%	+26%	+4%	-38%

In fact, on Tuesday May 7th 1963, for the whole day, only 93 people disembarked the trains arriving at Ilfracombe station, and just 346 people in total used the Barnstaple to Ilfracombe line during that day (embarking and disembarking from the various stations along the line).

all statistics, source: The Ilfracombe Line by John Nicholas

Such statistics make for gloomy reading but illustrate very well the drivers of the closures called for in the well-known "Dr. Beeching Report" of 27th March 1963. That the Ilfracombe Line survived for another 7 years was perhaps surprising; but, perhaps too, it was a reflection of the enduring (albeit diminishing) popularity of the railway to deliver tourists for their annual holiday.

Ultimately, of course, the car was ubiquitous; by the 1970s that, more than anything, doomed the branch and rural railways to closure: the car was king. "The man in the street" could quite literally drive from his home to his holiday accommodation, and do so on roads which were generally much more free of traffic than the roads of today.

What happened to the rural railways as a consequence? Convenience is what happened. Just hop in the car outside your home and go directly to your destination (be it work or holiday).

For the rural dweller the choice was even easier:

Why walk one or two miles or, in many cases, even further to a rural railway station sometimes located far from the nearest village (such being dictated by topography - trains don't travel up or down hills), and also endure the cold and the rain of winter whilst getting there to go to work?

Why go and fetch shopping, for example, by train when you can simply step into your car and load the boot to bring it home?

Who would, sensibly, choose the train?

Convenience and cost are the two drivers of choice, and convenience probably the paramount one in many instances.

The effect on such railways as the Ilfracombe Line (for example) was also a reflection of the sense of individual freedom: the freedom of the car, the freedom to decide where to stop *en route*, the facility to carry all necessary personal baggage (and the dog); and perhaps too the freedom from state control and bureaucracy *etc*.

A similar revolution was happening concurrently with **commercial goods transportation**; convenience once again dictated change: load the van or the lorry at your own premises and it will go direct to your customer, and at very reasonable cost.

How could the train compete?

It could not, except for the movement of fundamental industrial products in large volumes such as stone, coal, oil *etc*. The result, inevitable as it seems with hindsight, was a massive drop in the use of the train for freight.

Railway operating losses rose and rose some more, until the government could no longer see valid justification for the ever-increasing subsidy of rail. Along came Dr Beeching in 1963, and the cuts - extreme that they were - eventuated.

Hence, the major changes in the everyday life of society in general (the increases in personal income and in car mobility) had ultimately decided the fate of the relatively rural railway lines. The heyday of the railways was over.

What remains today, in the South-West most particularly, is the arterial or mainline route from Paddington to Penzance plus a few lesser lines serving the periphery of the major cities, and little else.

Most people and certainly the more rural vast majority of people in northern Devon and North Cornwall are without a railway unless they travel a *not inconsiderable* distance to access a station.

Is that still appropriate to life in the emerging trends of the 21st century as we begin to see and understand them?

The 19th century railways were a revolution for UK transport, for the UK population and its social norms, but they have largely been gone for 60 years. They lasted for about a hundred years, and there is now a second transport revolution happening before our eyes, right now: petroleum-based fuels are ceding to electricity for cars. Perhaps this is better described as an evolution, for the popularity of car ownership, whilst moderating noticeably, shows no sign of diminishing. Nevertheless, the switch to electricity is most certainly gaining momentum. Electric car range is increasing and range anxiety is, correspondingly, diminishing; but, even so, there remains concern about recharging availability; indeed, for persons living in (certainly first floor and above) flats - where they have no charging capability at home - an attractive solution is still not apparent; yet petrol and diesel-fuelled cars will be banned from 2030. Of course, this trend solely by itself is most unlikely to trigger a rush to the train sufficient for substantial investment justification.

The internal combustion engines of the car are now facing their demise, also after about a hundred years, but significant questions remain:

Will electric replacements satisfactorily serve the UK population?

Where is all the necessary electricity to come from?

How long will it take for a car charging supply network to proliferate?

Will such infrastructure serve rural Devon and Cornwall adequately?

It is also perhaps timely to consider the existing road infrastructure and the apparent satiation of the market for car ownership: almost all of those people who aspire to own a car have now, presumably, bought one; yet 20% of UK households do *not* own a car.

That 20% is, presumably principally, the very poorest of households, but it is also those city dwellers who consider a car unnecessary within their (dense) urban location.

Is it, for example, necessary, useful or even desirable to own a car when living in London with its excellent public transport and its punitive taxation tariffs on cars (the Congestion Zone, the Ultra Low Emission Zone)?

Only Londoners can decide for themselves, but many will opt not to own a car.

How are those 20% of the UK population without a car supposed to reach Ilfracombe (for example)?

At present, their choices would be to either hire a car or take one or more trains to Exeter and then a further train to Barnstaple, followed by a bus or taxi to Ilfracombe (carrying their luggage). They would have similar travel tribulations to reach other coastal towns such as Bude or Padstow.

Is such an itinerary appealing in a society seeking convenience?

Convenience or, strictly stated, the greater convenience of the car was the most influential factor in the demise of rural railways. It's important, indeed fundamental, to note that the author in this paper does not suggest that factor will be reversed; rather, this is a different perspective: restoring rural public transport should justify allowing rural house building, the land for which can be acquired very much more cheaply in order to create valuable open-market homes to sell to provide the source of funding for the required affordable homes.

If the relatively wealthier sectors of society stay with cheap flights to (warmer) foreign destinations and the relatively poorer folk who (presumably) own fewer cars have no rail access to Ilfracombe then who will visit?

This paper does not set out to be an analysis of the UK holiday and leisure market, but such is an essential element in considering restoration of 'lost' railways; indeed, it was railways that delivered ithe tourism heyday to Ilfracombe, and - *it could credibly be argued* - the town needs *something* to encourage investment generally. A restored railway connection would certainly help.

How are the staff who serve these coastal towns, which continue to have significance for tourists, to reach their place of employment? And parking spaces are few and costly. Worse: so is housing.

In summary, DaCSTaR intends to spark consideration of the fundamental problems of lack of housing and public transport within the South-West (northern Devon and north Cornwall more specifically at this stage), beginning with the transport defects of twenty-first century rural life and focusing on the potential merits of restoration of lost railway lines.

The questions that are presented are formidable and raise more:

Perhaps there is really little or no merit in such considerations?

Perhaps the railway is lost forever?

Has the increasing development of roads infrastructure met its congestion limits?

Has the saturation of ownership of the car reached its zenith, as the statistics suggest?

Could restored railway lines, once again, deliver a travel solution to he poorer segments of society as the increasing costs of everyday life bear down on them?

How could we, will we and when will we actually know the answers?

Definitive, credible answers are not within the remit or capabilities of the author and this paper. Doubtless, all of these questions will be hotly debated and opinions extremely diverse. However, the reader is asked to consider whether there are genuine alternatives to **a start** to a resolution of the major and fundamental difficulties which the South-West faces if it is ever to emerge from its long-held status as a 'backwater' in economic terms, with inadequate housing stock and a rising level of homelessness. It is surely time to embrace substantive and radical change, else where will our children live?

The lost lines: Where were they? Who did they serve?

The lost lines were, simply stated:

1.   Barnstaple to Ilfracombe;

2.   Barnstaple to Lynton (only ever a slow, narrow gauge, steam railway);

3.   Barnstaple to Dulverton (the westerly half of the Devon and Somerset Railway, and a junction with the line to Tiverton);

4.   Dulverton to Taunton (easterly half of the Devon and Somerset Railway), a link to the main line;

5.   The *northern* Exe Valley: Dulverton to Tiverton, plus a continuation with the other Tiverton line to the former Tiverton *Junction* station on the mainline *(the present Tiverton Parkway is not the perfect station for Tiverton, the town)*;

6.   The original or *southern* Exe Valley Railway: Tiverton to Stoke Canon - to link with the main line near Exeter;

7.   Barnstaple, via Bideford, to Torrington;

8.   Torrington to Halwill Junction;

9.   Bude to Halwill Junction;

10.   Launceston to Halwill Junction;

11.   Launceston to Padstow (The North Cornwall Line);

12.   Padstow to Bodmin;

13.   Halwill Junction to Okehampton;

14.   Okehampton to Tavistock (former Tavistock *North* station) and Bere Alston (connecting with the service to Plymouth);

15.   Launceston to Tavistock (former Tavistock *South* station);

16.   Tavistock *South* station to Marsh Mills (for Plymouth);

17.   Yelverton to Princetown.

see the diagrammatic network schema

The maximum potential for restoration of lost railway lines

The maximum potential for restoration on the track-bed of former lines is set out on the network schema as 17 separate but linked lines, recognising the likelihood that any such restorations will be piecemeal before the maximum possible outcome of restoration of all of them (*which is perhaps optimistic*).

Each of the 17 is accorded a different colour. All the former stations and halts are indicated. Those indicated in grey rather than black may conceivably not justify re-opening, particularly so in the modern day era where many people will drive to a particular (larger) station where they intend to board the train.

Barnstaple to Taunton via Dulverton, historically, operated as one line: the Devon and Somerset Railway. Dulverton provided a junction with the railway to Tiverton and further south down the Exe Valley to Exeter.

The suggested names for the different lines are the author's creations in the majority of cases; in others, the names have a historical pedigree.

Note that on the network schema the former North Cornwall Railway between Launceston and Padstow is proposed to terminate at Wadebridge. The reasons for this are fourfold:

- Single track railway lines are operated with one locomotive/train as a simple safety measure. However, this works only as far as it is possible to do so to achieve a sensible timetable. Longer lines with a solitary train would result in too great a time gap between departures - the original departure station would be waiting for too long for the returning solitary train;

- The bridge over the Little Petherick Creek just outside Padstow is wide enough for only a single-track railway;

- Transiting modern day Wadebridge for even a single track will be a challenge, and the limit of one track carrying the Bodmin train (on to Padstow) is deemed to be enough of a challenge *for a first stage* service;

- Of course, trains running in both directions can be managed on single-track lines, but in the stated aims of simplicity, the frequent services from Bodmin to Padstow could adequately serve to collect and deposit passengers alighting from northern Cornwall at Wadebridge.

Naturally, such a termination of the line could easily be reviewed if, as, and when, the two lines were established.

Note too that the former Devon and Somerset Railway between Barnstaple and Taunton is split into two lines. this is also an *initial stage* of operation and reflects too that one half of the whole line might conceivably be restored ahead of the other half. As per the reasons above (i.e. the Wadebridge terminus for the Launceston to Padstow line), this split in the Barnstaple - Taunton railway line could be reviewed and the two lines consolidated into one, once both are established. The example timetables within this document illustrate both possibilities.

A restored network of rural railway lines, a design schema.

17 individual lines.

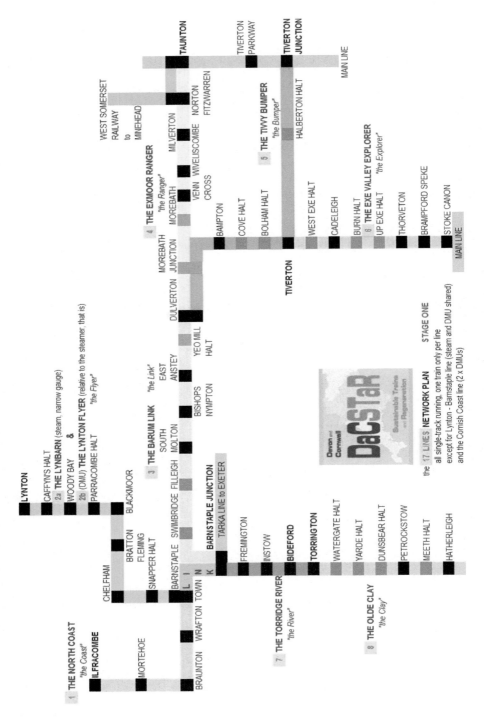

1 THE NORTH COAST
"the Coast"

2a THE LYNBARN (steam, narrow gauge)
&
2b (DMU) THE LYNTON FLYER (relative to the steamer that is)
"the Flyer"

3 THE BARUM LINK
"the Link"

4 THE EXMOOR RANGER
"the Ranger"

5 THE TIVVY BUMPER
"the Bumper"

6 THE EXE VALLEY EXPLORER
"the Explorer"

7 THE TORRIDGE RIVER
"the River"

8 THE OLDE CLAY
"the Clay"

LYNTON
CAFFYN'S HALT
WOODY BAY
PARRACOMBE HALT
BLACKMOOR
CHELFHAM
BRATTON FLEMING
SNAPPER HALT
ILFRACOMBE
MORTEHOE
BRAUNTON
WRAFTON
BARNSTAPLE TOWN
BARNSTAPLE
LINK
BARNSTAPLE JUNCTION
TARKA LINE to EXETER
SWIMBRIDGE
FILLEIGH
SOUTH MOLTON
BISHOPS NYMPTON
EAST ANSTEY
YEO MILL HALT
DULVERTON
MOREBATH
MOREBATH JUNCTION
BAMPTON
COVE HALT
BOLHAM HALT
TIVERTON
WEST EXE HALT
CADELEIGH
BURN HALT
UP EXE HALT
THORVERTON
BRAMPFORD SPEKE
STOKE CANON
MAIN LINE
VENN CROSS
WIVELISCOMBE
MILVERTON
NORTON FITZWARREN
TAUNTON
TIVERTON PARKWAY
TIVERTON JUNCTION
HALBERTON HALT
MAIN LINE
WEST SOMERSET RAILWAY to MINEHEAD
FREMINGTON
INSTOW
BIDEFORD
TORRINGTON
WATERGATE HALT
YARDE HALT
DUNSBEAR HALT
PETROCKSTOW
MEETH HALT
HATHERLEIGH

the **17** LINES **NETWORK PLAN**   **STAGE ONE**
all single-track running, one train only per line
except for Lynton - Barnstaple line (steam and DMU shared)
and the Cornish Coast line (2 x DMUs)

Devon and Cornwall
DaCSTaR
Sustainable Trains and Regeneration

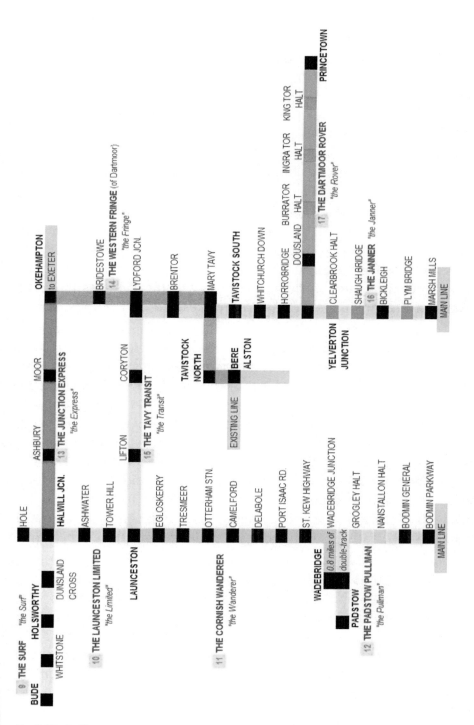

BUDE

9 **THE SURF** "the Surf"
HOLSWORTHY

WHITSTONE

DUNSLAND CROSS

HOLE

ASHBURY

MOOR

OKEHAMPTON

to EXETER

HALWILL JCN.

13 **THE JUNCTION EXPRESS**
"the Express"

ASHWATER

TOWER HILL

LIFTON

CORYTON

BRIDESTOWE

14 **THE WESTERN FRINGE** (of Dartmoor)
"the Fringe"

LYDFORD JCN.

BRENTOR

MARY TAVY

LAUNCESTON

10 **THE LAUNCESTON LIMITED**
"the Limited"

15 **THE TAVY TRANSIT**
"the Transit"

TAVISTOCK NORTH

TAVISTOCK SOUTH

WHITCHURCH DOWN

EGLOSKERRY

TRESMEER

OTTERHAM STN.

CAMELFORD

DELABOLE

PORT ISAAC RD.

ST. KEW HIGHWAY

11 **THE CORNISH WANDERER**
"the Wanderer"

BERE ALSTON

EXISTING LINE

HORROBRIDGE

BURRATOR HALT

DOUSLAND HALT

INGRATOR HALT

KING TOR HALT

PRINCETOWN

17 **THE DARTMOOR ROVER**
"the Rover"

CLEARBROOK HALT

SHAUGH BRIDGE

YELVERTON JUNCTION

WADEBRIDGE

0.8 miles of double-track

GROGLEY HALT

NANSTALLON HALT

BODMIN GENERAL

BODMIN PARKWAY

PADSTOW

12 **THE PADSTOW PULLMAN**
"the Pullman"

WADEBRIDGE JUNCTION

16 **THE JANNER** "the Janner"

BICKLEIGH

PLYM BRIDGE

MARSH MILLS

MAIN LINE

MAIN LINE

In north Devon, Barnstaple (Barnstaple Junction as it was known in its heyday) was the historical railway hub for many lines, including the *existing* link to Exeter *(the Tarka Line)*. Further south, Halwill Junction similarly acted as hub for lines heading north, south, east and west. In Cornwall, Launceston served as hub for the famous "North Cornwall Railway" with its rail link going east to Tavistock and thence to Plymouth; and another going south-west to Padstow to serve the fish and tourism industries, a branch of the famous **"Atlantic Coast Express"**.

Were it not for the dramatic economic realities revealed publicly by the Dr Beeching report of 1963, it might seem inconceivable that such an expansive extent of public infrastructure should be simply abandoned; worse: extents of it have been sold off, and other encroachments by such unlawful methods as simple possession have broken the integrity of the links in many places.

Contrary to popular misconception, the now infamous Beeching Report *per se* did **not** doom so many railway lines to closure; rather, lack of use did that: there were insufficient passengers and revenue to sustain rising costs. The government of the day deemed it unjustifiable to subsidise such unprofitable railways; indeed, borrowing money to sustain *operational* costs is never sensible unless a tangible turnaround, a *significant uplift in revenues*, is visible in the relatively short term; and this is more usually *not* the case for individuals, companies and the state; indeed, pursuing such a course of action as borrowing to fund operations might be expected to customarily lead to bankruptcy for individuals, insolvency for companies, and inflation and currency devaluation for states *(as is the case in the UK at the present time)*.

Hence, both at the time (the early 1960s) and with hindsight, railway line closures were simply unavoidable. The tragedy was that the track-beds and station locations were not preserved in perpetuity, saved for a *potential* future date when the economic, social and/or environmental situation might be more favourable. Unfortunately, track-beds and station locations have been sold off, redeveloped and perhaps lost forever; but is the situation really so bleak? This document explores that question.

The network 'schema' or map of the lost lines *(in the region in question, i.e. northern Devon and north Cornwall)* illustrates all of them and shows them as individual lines. A *tentative and prospective* name of identity has been proposed for each one.

It can be seen that they offered a widely-distributed network of lines which served to some degree at least the vast majority of the populace in the northern areas of Cornwall and Devon; as such they served both the *local* population (for commuting, for example, and for shopping, to reach the urban centres) and they were a foundation for *incoming tourists*, of whom virtually all did not possess a car when the railway network reached its peak and for many years thereafter.

In the 1930s, in the late 1940s after the war, and during the 1950s the *journey* by train from the industrial heartlands of the UK to the sunshine, sea and sandy beaches of the far distant south-west must *in itself* have seemed paradisiacal!

Nobody could have described that journey *(and its sad loss)* better than Sir John Betjeman himself in (a moving extract from) *"Summoned by Bells"*, his blank verse autobiography first published in 1960:

> *"And those young twins,*
> *Free Thought and clean Fresh Air:*
> *Attend the long express from Waterloo*
> *That takes us down to Cornwall. Tea-time shows*
> *The small fields waiting, every blackthorn hedge*
> *Straining inland before the south-west gale.*
> *The emptying train, wind in the ventilators,*
> *Puffs out of Egloskerry to Tresmeer*
> *Through minty meadows, under bearded trees*
> *And hills upon whose sides the clinging farms*
> *Hold Bible Christians. Can it really be*
> *That this same carriage came from Waterloo?*
> *On Wadebridge station what a breath of sea*
> *Scented the Camel valley! Cornish air,*
> *Soft Cornish rains, and silence after steam..."*

What a wonderful use of words; one can imagine being there!

The lost lines: Who might they serve, if restored?

The population of **Devon's** largest nineteen towns and cities (with a population in excess of 10,000) in 2011 was as follows:

	population	served by rail?	tourist destination? *
		in the sense of the traditional or historic, family week's holiday	
Plymouth	256,384	yes	no
Exeter	117,773	yes and by air	no
Torquay	65,245	yes	yes
Paignton	49,021	yes	yes
Exmouth	34,432	yes	yes
Barnstaple	24,033	yes	no
Newton Abbot	24,029	yes	no
Tiverton	21,335	no	no
Brixham	16,693	no	yes
Bideford	16,610	no	no
Teignmouth	14,749	yes	yes
Sidmouth	13,737	no	yes
Dawlish	13,161	yes	yes
Tavistock	12,280	no	no
Northam	12,062	no	no
Ivybridge	11,851	yes	no
Ilfracombe	11,509	no	yes
Honiton	11,156	yes	no
Kingsteignton	10,451	no	no
s/t	736,511		

North Devon has an extremely limited rail connection, from Barnstaple (only) to Exeter.

No tourist destination in **north Devon** is (well) served by rail. Every person arriving by train requires a transport change at Barnstaple.

8 of 19 (42%) of Devon's larger towns have <u>no</u> rail link.

62% (736,511) of Devon's total population of 1,194,166 (in 2019) is living in the larger conurbations (towns and cities) of which 621,837 or 84% of the population of these 19 larger towns have a rail link. This means that <u>just 52% of Devon's overall population has a rail link</u>.

The population of **Cornwall's** eleven largest towns (i.e. ones over 10,000 people) in 2021 was as follows:

	population	served by rail?		tourist destination?
St. Austell	27,400	yes		no
Falmouth	22,300	yes		yes
Camborne	21,600	yes		no
Penzance & Newlyn	21,200	yes		yes
Truro	21,000	yes		no
Newquay	20,300	yes	and by air	yes
Saltash	16,600	yes		no
Redruth	15,600	yes		no
Bodmin	15,300	yes		no
Helston	11,900	no		yes
St. Ives	11,500	yes		yes
s/t	**204,700**...			

... being 36% of Cornwall's total population of 568,200 (in 2021) of which only 192,800 or 34% of Cornwall's population (in these larger towns) have a rail link.

In Devon and Cornwall the five towns of Tiverton, Bideford, Tavistock, Northam and Kingsteignton are not served by rail and nor are they traditional tourist destinations.

Northern Cornwall has no rail connection whatsoever.

Of the thirty largest towns and cities in the Devon and Cornwall peninsula (with a population of over 10,000), nine (30%) have no rail link; fourteen are tourist attractions (47%); and of those fourteen tourist destinations ten (71%) <u>do</u> have a rail link and 4 <u>do not</u> (29%)

Only the tourist towns of Ilfracombe, Brixham and Sidmouth (all 3 in Devon) and Helston (in Cornwall) have <u>no</u> rail link.

In considering the attributes, merits and disadvantages applicable to each of the *above* towns, the conclusion that seems perfectly obvious to the author is that the *following* towns would benefit from the restoration of a rail link: Tiverton, Bideford, Tavistock, Northam and Kingsteighton; all of which have no <u>nearby</u> rail connection.

Arguably, Tiverton Parkway might be considered to provide rail access to Tiverton (the town), but this necessitates <u>driving</u> on the A361 to the M5 at Junction 27 for the nearby Parkway station or taking the 'back road' on a relatively slow drive through villages *en route*. Hence Tiverton Parkway cannot be said to adequately serve those Tiverton people (or anyone else) *without a car*; of course, a taxi is an option for some but unaffordable for others.

Arguably too, Kingsteignton might be considered to be in such close proximity to Newton Abbot that it benefits from that town's rail station.

Similarly, the close proximity of Northam to Bideford suggests that a restored single rail connection to Bideford could be utilised by both towns (Northam is, essentially, a residential adjunct to Bideford).

Which leads to a conclusion - *a standout case* - primarily, for restoration of rail links to both Bideford and Tavistock.

And as Torrington is so very close to Bideford, it would seem eminently sensible to continue a restored railway line (which starts) from Barnstaple, continues to Bideford and thence onwards to Torrington.

Similarly, it would also seem sensible in the first instance to link Tavistock to Plymouth via Bere Alston, and also to Exeter via Okehampton; indeed, the latter route would provide an alternative when the existing mainline is severed by sea storms, as has happened on several occasions in relatively recent years. Devon County Council is pursuing the first part of this objective, Tavistock to Bere Alston.

Furthermore, the Devon **tourist** towns of **Ilfracombe**, **Brixham** and **Sidmouth** (the latter two being outside the **DaCSTaR** area of this document) can also be considered to be prime candidates for rail restoration, which would certainly aid their economies. In <u>north</u> Devon, <u>the subject of this document</u>, Ilfracombe is therefore the secondary candidate after Bideford (with extension to Torrington).

In Cornwall, of the larger towns, **Helston** (as a tourist town, but outside the present **DaCSTaR** area of this document) stands out as a prime candidate for rail restoration. However, the traditional (albeit smaller) tourist towns of **Bude** and **Padstow** in <u>northern</u> Cornwall (the subject of this document) must also merit positive consideration, as such would restore some semblance of rail connectivity to the wider region of northern Cornwall as well as aid the tourist economies of both those towns.

Restoration: Lost causes? A pipe dream or not?

There are certainly lost segments of closed railway lines which would be problematical to restore. For example: in North Devon, the track-bed of the rail line towards Taunton was used to build the A361 North Devon Link Road between Barnstaple and South Molton; and the vicinity of the former station at Tiverton and its approaches for the railway have been lost to an inner bypass road.

Yet, for the vast majority of the length of these lines, they are located in a rural environment; and it is most probable that the track-bed remains even now, after half a century since closure, because - for the most part - farmers would be unlikely to plough up the stone and gravel constituents of former railway track-bed as they would be reluctant to disperse it into their 'virgin' fields.

Certainly there are many challenges to restoration of any 'lost' railway line, but it must be borne in mind that what is postulated (and particularly so within the more urban areas) is a very narrow band or strip of land within which a single-track railway line 'fits', i.e. it does not consume a wide area of 'expensive' development land.

As such, it is not beyond the engineering capabilities of the construction industry to widen, where necessary, 'linking' roads (such as the A361 mentioned above) to create the ground conditions for a parallel railway line.

Indeed, if a restored line in relatively more urban areas was considered to be akin to the tram then feasibility of restoration does not seem so far-fetched.

Trams (on rails) are a common feature in many of the world's greatest cities: San Francisco and Amsterdam leap to mind; and although the tram might be somewhat lighter than a 'regular' train, the key attribute is the speed: trains can be slowed to no more than the conventional, relatively slow speed of a tram to transit urban environments. One addition which is adopted in some urban transport regimes is the 'cowcatcher' mounted on the front of the train/tram; indeed, when the early trains were bought for the Lynton - Barnstaple

Railway, a Baldwin locomotive imported from the USA had just that; and it was retained for the life of the railway.

A San Francisco street tram.   Photo: Bernard Mills.

There are other recent trends in UK life: The COVID pandemic has illustrated the feasibility of working from home; but is that a temporary response or will it endure, at least in part? And working from home hardly reinforces aspirations for railway restoration. Or does it? If the private car sees less use in travel to work, the pressing need to have one is, to a degree, diminished; but not entirely. Can the train fill that diminished necessity for travel?

It's important to recall that convenience remains the key driver for decision-making in respect of transportation; it supersedes cost concerns for most people. No train service, as good as it might be, can ever approach the car for convenience - until the car journey itself becomes inconvenient or costly. A train service could, conceivably, better the private car for cost; but only where the need for transportation is extremely narrowly defined: the trip from a nearby station into a not-too-distant workplace, for example; but private use will always be more varied and necessary; so the train cannot fulfil every modern life requirement; it's impossible.

Why on earth, therefore, should anyone believe that a reversal of (at least some of) the historic cuts to railway lines would be sensible?

In considering the role for the train, the widest evaluation of every conceivable purpose is necessary; and, of course, the primary purpose will vary from place to place: for example, very few people will travel by train from the more remote rural locations where they live to those places (generally a half-hour to an hour away by car) where they work. In the first instance, many people will not have access to a train station much nearer than simply driving all the way to work. However, such rural train lines as might be reinstated will certainly bring those tourists with a fascination for the railways; the simple fact of restoration will promote huge interest.

Will it be enough to sustain train operations? By itself, probably not. No single factor will sustain train operating costs as they were and are presently. **First**, it is essential to consider every conceivable purpose for each individual train line; **second**, it is essential to consider how costs can be minimised.

In respect of commercial goods, a train renaissance seems less likely than one for people. In respect of people, trains may be used for commuting, for personal travel and for tourism. As stated above, it seems unlikely that personal travel by itself will underpin the viability of trains: the extensive variety of personal travel and the unavailability or at least the inconvenience of the train for the majority of personal travel purposes militates against the train. Commuting is a more valid rationale, as is tourism.

For example, Ilfracombe, Bude and Padstow, in the past, received large volumes of tourists by train; holidaymakers travelled in their thousands (indeed, in their tens of thousands) every Saturday to these resorts. The famous **Atlantic Coast Express** travelled directly to these resorts from London's Waterloo station. These days, the majority of holidaymakers will own a car; and when they arrive, they will also wish to get about to see neighbouring places and attractions, which still militates against the train.

Cheap air travel to warmer climes also further ravaged tourist numbers as the 1970s unfolded. How can Ilfracombe or Bude compete with Majorca, or even such far flung places as Mexico, for the more adventurous? What do Ilfracombe and Bude have which is competitive?

Padstow has to some extent demonstrated how: the huge success and popularity of Rick Stein's fish catering enterprises now fills the town in the summer; indeed, it does in the spring and autumn too. The author visited in mid-September after walking some way along the 'Camel Trail', and the town quayside and its car park were filled to capacity; however, the road to reach the town is far from ideal; indeed, how well it copes with peak summer traffic levels is debatable.

Can other such north Devon and north Cornwall coastal resorts ever regain such widespread popularity as they enjoyed in the fifties? No one who has been to St. Ives in the summer would doubt it; indeed, St. Ives by car is a veritable nightmare, both for the tourist striving to park a car and also for the locals of the town who see their limited parking capacity appropriated by the tourist. At least there remains a branch railway into the town. Padstow is not far behind the popularity of St. Ives; indeed, the huge driving force that Rick Stein has proved to be might be said to have rejuvenated the entire town. St. Ives thrives on art, Padstow on fish (eating it); Bude, to a degree, has an appeal to surfers (Widemouth Bay certainly does); Ilfracombe in recent years has also looked towards art and benefited to some degree by the presence of Damien Hirst's interests; indeed, his 'Verity' statue is a spectacular and most positive step for the promotion of the town; it is somewhat disappointing that more artists have not followed in his steps.

After two years of strict lockdown, the author booked a week on the Algarve for April 2022, in hope that COVID might relent by then. The cost of a return flight from Bristol to Faro was a mere £38. I booked a first-class hotel and I planned to travel from Faro airport on the local train to the town where I wished to stay. I intended to spend a week walking, simply walking, and with a camera. I had no intentions of hiring a car, I intended to walk everywhere I wished to go, which meant relatively near to the town (along beaches and through salt marshes).* Therein lies the clue for the success of resort tourism and trains: the destination must (largely) appeal as a (largely) standalone attraction; there must be good dining, good accommodation and a fundamental element which captures the interest of the tourist.

Unfortunately, COVID did not relent and the holiday did not happen.

Could the train itself be that essential attraction for the promotion of tourism throughout Devon and Cornwall?

Certainly so, for 'trainspotters', but possibly so too for a wider interest if the destinations themselves were to hold an inherent appeal. For example, it is not difficult to believe that Padstow might once again be an attractive destination for a new **"Atlantic Coast Express"**.

A more expansive rail tour might be a feasible basis for wider exploration of the coast and countryside of the south-west peninsula. Therein lies one pointer to bringing about the rejuvenation of rail and the regeneration of the peninsula's economy: all local Planning Authorities must be supportive throughout the peninsula, supporting planning applications for tourist accommodation, for art galleries and for bars and restaurants *etc* (ones where the public is actually permitted to drive to them). Indeed, national authority must also be fundamentally supportive because closed branch lines will require an Act of Parliament if they are to be reinstated; and without such a national policy framework, nothing can be achieved.

More on this later.

The present state of track-beds, bridges, tunnels, obstructions, alternatives

There are a number of in-print books about the lost lines (see appendices) which offer splendid photographs and describe the state-of-play of the lost lines as they are today. Hence; for the first draft of this document it is not a subject described in detail. In brief:

- the tunnels on the lost lines, generally stated, still exist and are in fine fettle;
- some of the bridges across rivers and roads still exist, although a number have been wholly demolished, and others serve either road or pedestrian purposes;
- the majority of the more rural track-bed, for the most part, still exists; albeit there are some significant exceptions; for example, the Barnstaple to South Molton section of the A361 North Devon Link Road;
- more urban areas present a greater challenge where the track-bed has been built upon; such construction includes both roads and buildings; for example, the location of and close approach to the lost Tiverton station is now under a bypass road*; Braunton has a small block of flats adjacent to the lost line; the former line at Barnstaple Town (from Ilfracombe) is straddled by a small block of flats, and although there is a small 'tunnel' underneath the first floor of them through which a DMU might just squeeze, that does not seem a solution likely to find support from the residents.

in Tiverton, there is sufficient land to restore a rail line alongside the new southern bypass road; the bridge to the west over the Exe could share road and rail with suitable traffic lights.

It must be borne in mind that there are several factors which ameliorate and justify finding alternatives and solutions to these restoration obstructions; the railway offers the opportunity:

- to generate wealth (see: funding, below),
- to create employment,

- to offer environmentally-friendly transportation (relative to the car and even zero emissions when electric-driven trains become a viable prospect),
- to generate industry and commerce, *and*
- to help resolve the region's major housing problem
  (see: funding, below).

For all these substantial reasons, some road diversions (aside from the A361 section mentioned above) are quite short in length and worth making the changes. Similarly, relocation of some development (residential and other) is also sensible in order to achieve the substantial benefits for the region.

The lost lines: trains, stations and halts, length of lines, potential users, timetables

The listed restored rail lines are identified with suggested line names (always an aid to marketing and popularity). The postulated timetables are founded on those of the last years of the lost railways, it being assumed that those lines and operators had achieved maximum efficiency in their operation, even with steam trains. A switch to more modern train types (as below) and a simplification (as postulated) in track layouts (no reintroduction of freight trains is considered, for example) might likely enable modest incremental improvements on the passenger timetables of the 1960s, but in all probability they would only be modest.

A suggested timetable for a modern diesel train to serve Lynton is entirely the author's creation.

In those last years of the lost lines the era of steam was drawing to a close; steam locomotives were being replaced by diesels. For passenger trains on branch lines the standard or common format of train was the Diesel Multiple Unit ("DMU"). The advantage of this train type was that it could go forwards or backwards, there was a driver's cab at both ends of the train. Hence, unlike a steam locomotive (or even a diesel one), the DMU did not require (a) a turntable upon which a locomotive could be turned round (to go in the opposite direction) nor (b) a parallel length of track by which a locomotive could run around the train's coaches from one end to the other (a "runaround loop") so as to lead the train when it ran in the other direction to return to the other end of the line it served. The operating advantages of the DMU were so favourable that it became ubiquitous, and it exists today on all branch lines (the Tarka Line, for example).

Furthermore, the DMU, with its front and back cabs, could be linked with any number of intermediate coaches in order to suit the passenger demand on a particular line. Indeed, the smallest version of the DMU was not, strictly a multiple unit; it consisted of a single vehicle with a driver's cab at each end.

For more on the DMU see: *https://railcar.co.uk/technology/the-basics/*

A three-coach DMU; diesel power such as this is the likely commuter train for Devon's long rural lines; however, it could ultimately be switched to electric. Single-coach trains would likely predominate on many lines; however, the arrangement offers 1, 2, 3 and more coaches as required, and so is very versatile. Photo: Bernard Mills.

This paper (and the railway lines which are described herein) is based solely on passenger travel; as such and to facilitate the greatest possible appeal to the most widespread audience - people who are being asked to consider travelling by rail and not by their car - the entirety of all historical stations and halts is included, however small. The DMU trains are, essentially and principally, commuter trains for local people in a far ranging and rural region, currently almost entirely with a total absence of trains; secondly, they will offer an appeal to tourists, people who are not commuting and who are not pressed to seek the saving of ten, twenty or thirty minutes; people who have set their minds on the search for relaxation. As such, the lines to be restored - in adopting the 'old' timetables - offer relatively slow trains in comparison to the road speed of a car; however, the train does not halt in traffic jams, and neither does it incur a delay (and fee) for car parking. Hence, even at the speed of the regulatory maximum of "Light Railways" (35 mph), which many of the lost railways actually were, the train can compete with the car for almost all relatively shorter journeys.

Of course, were these lines restored, in practice the use of some halts might prove to be not worthwhile; a lack of demand might deem them to be 'stop on demand' halts (the modern technology to enable that surely exists today).

Simplicity and the lowest cost budget in every respect are paradigms of this proposal. Leaving aside freight and restoring lines solely for passengers offers great simplicity; this can be adopted in the design of track layouts overall and in station layouts too.

The principal type of train postulated is the DMU. In simple terms it will go from the buffer stops at one end of the line it serves to the buffer stops at the other end of the line, where it will simply reverse to travel the return journey. In many (indeed, most) cases, this is the operational strategy and design. A simple operation such as that described needs no signal boxes, no lineside signals, no points (or switches as they are also known), and so has a greatly lesser operating and maintenance cost, and a higher safety margin.

Of course, the total simplicity as described is not always feasible. The network schema illustrates a layout which has a visual resemblance to the London Tube plan; this is by intention: in a restored south-west network of branch lines, for local people a great deal of their journeys will tend to be the shorter, commuter-type journeys, for which (as is the case on the Tube) people are prepared to change trains/lines at an intermediate station on their route. There is nothing akin to the lengthy rail routes of the past (one example being the Wolverhampton to Ilfracombe through train on Saturdays).

The proposed restored network is precisely that: a network, a comprehensive one. A railway line running from A to B and a second one from C to D is greatly disadvantaged if there is no rail link between B and C.

It may be stating the obvious, but the point is that a *comprehensive* network is essential if restored rail lines are to be successful; and this has implications for the management of every restored line *(more on that below)*.

The last operating timetables of the various historical lines have been used to devise an illustration of potential future timetables, which follow. There are two exceptions:

(1) Barnstaple to Lynton aboard a steam train travelling at 15mph would not be palatable to commuters going to and from work, nor would it appeal to the 'more mainstream' tourist; hence a new timetable for a DMU has been created; however, the narrow-gauge steam train line has also been perpetuated, and its timetable is shown. In the latter case, the steam train terminates at Barnstaple Town (restored to service) whilst the DMU continues to connect with other lines at Barnstaple Junction (the present station with its original name also restored). *More on both trains below.*

(2) The line between Torrington and Halwill Junction was always slow. Built to a lesser standard of construction as a 'Light Railway' and meandering somewhat to serve a politically-driven route in order to serve the village of Hatherleigh, the lengthy travel time between the two stations (one hour twenty-three minutes at best for a journey of just under 21 miles; 15 mph) would also be unappealing to commuters and tourists. Hence, a timetable with the train speed increased (to 25 mph) and the time considerably reduced is postulated.

A restored Ilfracombe-Barnstaple line would enable:

1.   commuters to travel between the two towns,
2.   Ilfracombe residents (who may have no car) to affordably reach the North Devon capital of Barnstaple (including the hospital),
3.   Ilfracombe residents to make onward rail journeys to the rest of the country,
4.   tourists to reach Ilfracombe by rail.

A new Ilfracombe station (atop the hill)* would require easy access from and to the town (by bus and taxi) and a car park at the station. Furthermore, the cost of car parking would require careful consideration if the benefits of train travel are not to be eroded to the point where the car persists. * *More on this later.*

The following timetables illustrate the scope and limitations of restored railway lines; their purpose is to stimulate the reader's thinking about the appeal and viability of rail versus road.

Unlike the car, timetables are necessary, and that dictates a relative paucity of choice in the timing of every journey; but on the other side of the coin there are advantages too: sitting in the train carriage and browsing on the laptop (or the phone) whilst enjoying a coffee will undoubtedly be more relaxing than enduring the traffic jam, driving in severe bad weather, finding a car parking space (and paying for it), and repeating the process on the way home.

The train is a very different animal to the car; indeed, it might be said that its advantages are almost forgotten after an era (in the south-west at least) of non-availability. The train for south-west people - *after the near total axing of all branch railway lines* - became a means of travel for only a tiny minority within the peninsula, perhaps used in the majority of instances **for business purposes to travel outside the region**, to London *etc*. A few commuter lines remain and the economics of these lines are not available to the author, but their inclusion would certainly be helpful to the discussion.

In the specific region on which this paper majors, there is a commendable success story:

"**The Tarka Line**'s fortunes have been transformed in recent decades. Where once there was concern for its very survival, the line now has its best ever service and unprecedented numbers of passengers, thanks to a lot of work by a lot of people over many years.

Working together, these (people) have secured the line's best ever service, attractive fares and a tripling of the number of passengers using the line – up from 200,000 in 2001 to nearly 680,000 in 2018."

source: https://dcrp.org.uk/lines/tarka-line/

In fact, the increase in passenger numbers on the Tarka Line has far exceeded that of the average (more modest) increase for UK branch lines. As a barometer for what could be achieved in the region for restored branch lines (principally serving commuters), there could not be a better example.

However, the proposals herein go further than restoration of branch lines *per se*; rather, whilst branch lines by themselves will give something of a boost to tourist numbers, this paper proposes to promote tourism with the addition of *heritage steam* trains operating on the restored branch lines alongside a modern commuter service. This is fundamental to the prospects of success of gaining substantially increased numbers of tourists throughout the region.

As stated above, **the following (illustrative) timetables** are essentially based on those *pre*-Beeching, with two exceptions: (1) the line between Torrington and Halwill Junction which managed only about 12 mph (a more appealing speed, one comparable to other branch lines, has been postulated), and (2) the Lynton-Barnstaple line is similarly postulated with a DMU, only ever having a narrow-gauge steam train which is entirely unsuitable for the people of Lynton and Lynmouth to commute to Barnstaple.

However, a restored line between Barnstaple and Lynton could also offer restored running for the narrow-gauge steamers of the tourist railway, sharing the line with a modern DMU *(more on that below)*. Doubtless that would present a few operational challenges, but it must be borne in mind that the generation of increased tourism in the region is one of the primary targets of this strategy, and certainly the 'steamer' running the full length of the line would be a great tourism asset.

All the restored branch lines would serve tourists and commuters, to a greater and lesser degree on the various lines; and so the proposed timetables offer departures with a frequency of no more than two hours, and usually less; and they also strive to avoid those times where such trains might be less used, late evenings for example, in order to minimise operational costs.

As a generality, commuter services' departures from regional towns to the 'capital', Barnstaple begin at 8am, with a final return departure time of about 7pm. Exceptions include, for example, the "Tivvy Bumper" (a popular name from the past) which returns from the Tiverton Junction (a restored link) to Tiverton town later in the evening so as to offer mainline travellers a return home to the town courtesy of the branch line.

The overall speed of the train journey in the 1950s and even the 1960s for these branch lines was not fast; typically, it averaged about 25mph (another factor which decided people in favour of the car). This paper does not care to suggest that more modern trains could go much faster: the railwaymen of those times had long experience and certainly knew what they were doing; they understood the capabilities and limitations of the railways.

However, the combination of a number of factors could well deliver relatively modest improvements on those times, including (for example):

1. for the most part the lines are operated with a single train and there is no need for measures which slow the train in order to prevent a risk of head-on collision;

2. modern technology such as GPS and far better mobile communications assist safety on those lines with more than a single train operating on single track lines;

3. road/rail crossings can be automated.

The following timetables are only first drafts, "thought-provokers" if you will; they illustrate the likely timing of the journeys for each line; however, they *would* require modification in order that passengers who switched from one line to another could avoid long waiting times for the next train on the next, onward stage of their journey *(the frequency of trains on every route generally being between one and two hours)*. Therein lies another of the advantages of the car over the train, one which must be overcome, or at least ameliorated, to the best possible extent.

At each station and halt there must also be services for passengers, including: toilets, shelter from weather, and refreshments *(more on that later)*.

Certainly, at each station a bus service to and from the town (centre) awaiting the arrival of every train would be highly desirable, possibly even an essential component of a service which must attain credibility with the public.

The following additional information on only *some* of the lost railway lines excludes the majority of them; it also does not seek to be all-inclusive, comprehensive, or sufficiently detailed to be able to form conclusions in any respect; it merely strives to show examples, ones which hopefully illustrate that solutions can usually be found for the, doubtless, substantial obstacles to restoration of the lost railway lines.

The author concludes that for such a program to be successful (in parts or in whole) then popular support will be a necessary precondition. The benefits to the people of the region are so very considerable that such support will surely be within reach; however, policymakers and influencers of all sorts must lead the way.

The Ilfracombe to Barnstaple Line: an example of a restored railway line.

Time is an important factor when considering the relative merits of the train versus the car, particularly so for the commuter. The postulated timetable *(previous page)* suggests a travel time from **Ilfracombe station to Barnstaple Town station** of 44 minutes for the 14.9 miles of the journey. It is a speed of only 20 mph. In addition, the commuter has to reach a restored Ilfracombe station from where he/she lives in the town.

How does this compare with the car?

The author drove the route on a November Saturday morning with very little traffic. From Barnstaple Town station to the site of the former Ilfracombe station took exactly 30 minutes; the subsequent walk from (near) the station site at the top of Station Street to the town High Street took 7 minutes. Bearing in mind that the tourist season was finished, such a trip was fast compared to a likely time throughout the summer, in the congestion of tourist traffic. The historic timetable train equivalent (station to station) was 44 minutes, a near 50% uplift on the car travel time; however, there is no time lost in parking a car at either end, and so this train time might likely be deemed acceptable, particularly so in these days of the 'connected' society with addiction to the internet (which would be available on the train); indeed, all things considered, the train begins to look appealing. The train commute does offer this significant advantage over the car: the commuter can be connected to the web, online in the comfort of his train seat.

One further factor is important in these comparisons: where does the commuter (or the tourist) actually start his/her journey? An Ilfracombe resident commuter, considering the train, has to gain the station. Atop quite a hill, the author walked for near double the time returning from the High St to the Ilfracombe station site (it's a steep hill). Hills are not appealing to older folk or those who are unfit or disabled. This aspect favours the car journey *or requires a bus*.

However, this paper remains mindful of the car becoming less affordable for many as the current day pressures mount (inflation, fuel, taxation, recessionetc) and bear down disproportionately on the less well off. All these factors lead towards two conclusions: vehicular access to a restored Ilfracombe Station would be necessary; whether by taxi or local bus, and car parking at the station would also be a *necessary* 'enabler' to take car traffic off the road to Barnstaple.

In respect of the siting of that parking and a new station, both factors would necessarily be influenced by the incumbent Pall factory owners and requirements. Whether they would voluntarily concede a part of their more remote staff parking zone to the south is the key question; a new station could be constructed a little to the south of its former location (the Pall factory) with no great loss of convenience to the rail traveller.

It must be borne in mind that a restored rail network would be extremely different from its historical predecessor, not least in the matter of the station; restored platforms would be simply that: *relatively small* platforms; a place with weather shelter at which to board and exit the train with, perhaps, a refreshment kiosk, i.e. simplistic structures. *See later for proposals for charging for travel.*

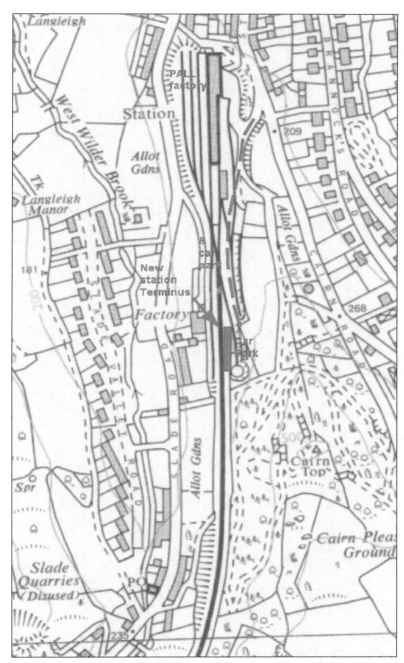

a new location for Ilfracombe station (platform)

The NORTH COAST — column "1"

The NORTH COAST	minutes	14.9	miles	20 mph	1 train	02:00	cycle
	en route	08:00	10:00	12:00	14:00	16:00	18:00
Ilfracombe - depart							
Mortehoe	10	08:10	10:10	12:10	14:10	16:10	18:10
Braunton	13	08:23	10:23	12:23	14:23	16:23	18:23
Wrafton	13	08:36	10:36	12:36	14:36	16:36	18:36
Barnstaple Town	8	08:44	10:44	12:44	14:44	16:44	18:44
Barnstaple river bridge	5	08:49	10:49	12:49	14:49	16:49	18:49
reverse	2	08:51	10:51	12:51	14:51	16:51	18:51
Barnstaple Junction - arrival	5	08:56	10:56	12:56	14:56	16:56	18:56
wait - before departure at	4	09:00	11:00	13:00	15:00	17:00	19:00
Barnstaple river bridge	5	09:05	11:05	13:05	15:05	17:05	19:05
reverse	2	09:07	11:07	13:07	15:07	17:07	19:07
Barnstaple Town	5	09:12	11:12	13:12	15:12	17:12	19:12
Wrafton	8	09:20	11:20	13:20	15:20	17:20	19:20
Braunton	13	09:33	11:33	13:33	15:33	17:33	19:33
Mortehoe	13	09:46	11:46	13:46	15:46	17:46	19:46
Ilfracombe - arrival	10	09:56	11:56	13:56	15:56	17:56	19:56
wait - before departure at	4	10:00	12:00	14:00	16:00	18:00	parked
	120						

Ilfracombe - Barnstaple Town: a recreation from the historic timetable

A bridge across the River Taw

Trains to and from both Lynton and Ilfracombe to Barnstaple, which might provide for connections at Barnstaple (Barnstaple *Junction*, that is; i.e. the present-day station) for travel further afield, require a bridge to cross the River Taw. The former bridge for these routes, which crossed the river alongside the existing Long (road) Bridge, is long gone; indeed, had it remained *in situ* during the decades since it was demolished it likely would have rusted away (regular maintenance would have seemed pointless after the Beeching cuts).

But how could trains travel from Barnstaple Town to Barnstaple Junction?

Fortunately, there is another river bridge, further upstream, which also served trains; it delivered the service to and from Taunton; and, thankfully, at the time of writing that bridge is undergoing further restoration.

cc-by-sa/2.0 - © Robin Drayton - geograph.org.uk/p/3063129

There is one (imaginative) potential route by which Ilfracombe and Lynton (regular) trains could reach the existing Barnstaple station *(which would be renamed Barnstaple Junction to differentiate it from a reinstated Barnstaple Town station)* using the existing Taw railway bridge. Such a route requires - *for both the Ilfracombe and Lynton lines -* its track laid:

- across a suitable or restored bridge over the mouth of the River **Yeo**, i.e. changes likely would be needed to the swing bridge
- along the former rail route (the present coastal path) to connect with North Walk; then in a sweeping curve to pass:
- along the (largely) vehicle-free Castle Street,
- across the north end of the Long Bridge approach - with traffic lights to halt the flow of cars; (the present lights could be moved slightly closer to the bridge), then
- across the paved square in front of the Museum of North Devon;

The train would then continue:

- along Taw Vale (the street river side) to the traffic roundabout,
- the line would then curve right to follow closely the **River Taw** on the edge of Rock Park,
- then the line would curve left (east and north) on a line parallel with the former railway bridge embankment, and join the railway line which is the one to Taunton*;
- from where the train would reverse, transit the **River Taw** on the existing railway bridge and continue the short distance to the existing Barnstaple (Junction) Station *(along the former Great Western Railway track route).*

*In fact, the existing River Taw bridge would also serve a restored rail line across Exmoor to reach Taunton (the route of the historic Devon and Somerset Railway, closed after the Beeching report). *More on that below.*

Thus, with an acceptance that a very slow urban train could be perceived <u>as a tram</u> for the transit between Barnstaple Town station and the River Taw bridge, no substantial expenditure would be required to construct a *new* rail bridge.

This Amsterdam street scene could almost be visualised as Barnstaple's Castle Street looking towards the Museum of North Devon in the distance; instead of the tram there would be a slow DMU train.

This photograph is licensed under the Creative Commons Attribution-Share Alike 2.5 Generic, 2.0 Generic and 1.0 Generic license.
Author: Meursault2004 aka Revo Arka Giri Soekatno

Trains in urban areas would be required to travel at no more than 15mph for safety, as do trams in many north European cities.

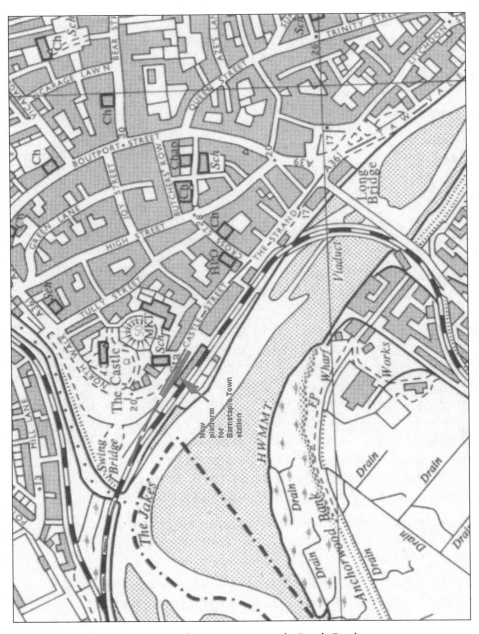

Train transit from Barnstaple Town towards Rock Park

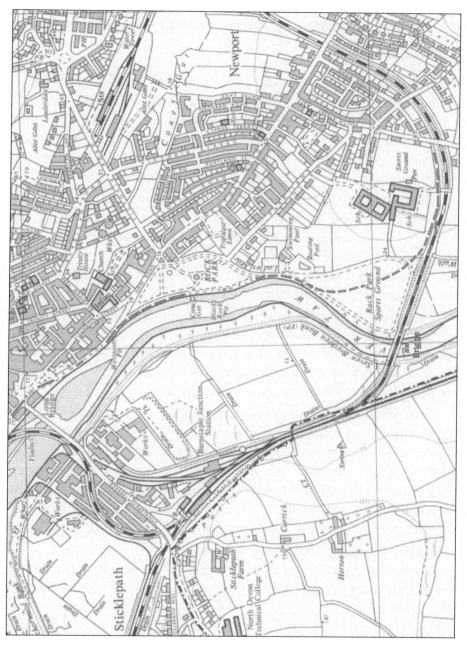

Transit from Barnstaple Town over the River Taw to Barnstaple Junction

The Lynton to Barnstaple Line: an example of a restored railway line.

The Lynton-Barnstaple Railway came late in the Great Railway Investment Revolution, the company being formed in 1895; the line was built and completed by 1898; but, sadly, it operated only until closure in 1935. Unlike its contemporaries it was always a narrow-gauge railway; there was never a subsequent 'regular' (in the sense of standard-gauge) railway line between Lynton and Barnstaple.

The short-lived narrow-gauge railway provided a slow service indeed. This may have been acceptable in the early decade or two of the 20th century, when few had access to a car; but the car surely doomed this enterprise: a time of 1 hour 38 minutes to travel 19 miles and at an average speed of about 13 mph was too slow, even by the relatively more relaxed standards of that time, 90 years ago.

The author drove the route on a November Saturday; the journey from Barnstaple Town station to Lynton Station took 34 minutes, admittedly in very little traffic - the tourist season having finished. The car shaved an hour off the historic time for the 'steamer'. It's probably a safe bet to say that it was more comfortable too.

One of the primary drivers of restored railway lines is the aspiration to boost tourist numbers throughout the region and more particularly to the 'traditional' resort towns which have declined relative to their 'heyday'. In this respect a (narrow-gauge) steam railway between Barnstaple Town (including restoration of that station, convenient for the town centre) and Lynton (the whole line restored) would certainly be a greatly appealing tourist attraction.

Wales, for example, possesses three of the top ten most scenic railway lines in Europe, exceeding the appeal of even the scenic mountain railways of Switzerland, according to a survey by **Which?** *More on this later.*

Restoration of the original route through the Pilton quarter of Barnstaple, whilst seemingly presenting insuperable problems, is certainly feasible when it is considered that a train interjecting into road traffic is a relatively infrequent event during the day; and the coexistence of car and train could be controlled with no more an obstacle or a physical separation than traffic lights.

2a - steam

The LYNBARN narrow gauge steam Southbound 19.3 miles	13 mph 2 trains 02:00 cycle					
	minutes Lynton to Barnstaple Town					
Lynton - departure	en route	09:00	11:00	13:00	15:00	17:00	19:00

	en route	09:00	11:00	13:00	15:00	17:00	19:00
Lynton - departure		09:00	11:00	13:00	15:00	17:00	19:00
Caffyn's Halt	9	09:09	11:09	13:09	15:09	17:09	19:09
Woody Bay	9	09:18	11:18	13:18	15:18	17:18	19:18
Parracombe Halt	9	09:27	11:27	13:27	15:27	17:27	19:27
Blackmoor	13	09:40	11:40	13:40	15:40	17:40	19:40
passing halt to allow DMU to pass	5	09:45	11:45	13:45	15:45	17:45	19:45
Bratton Fleming	18	10:03	12:03	14:03	16:03	18:03	20:03
Chelfham	15	10:18	12:18	14:18	16:18	18:18	20:18
Snapper Halt	9	10:27	12:27	14:27	16:27	18:27	20:27
Barnstaple Town	11	10:38	12:38	14:38	16:38	18:38	20:38
wait (coal and water) - departure at	22	11:00	13:00	15:00	17:00	19:00	parked
	120						

2a - steam

The LYNBARN narrow gauge steam Northbound 19.3 miles	13 mph 2 trains 02:00 cycle					
	minutes Barnstaple Town to Lynton					

	en route	09:00	11:00	13:00	15:00	17:00	19:00
Barnstaple Town - departure		09:00	11:00	13:00	15:00	17:00	19:00
Snapper Halt	11	09:11	11:11	13:11	15:11	17:11	19:11
Chelfham	9	09:20	11:20	13:20	15:20	17:20	19:20
passing halt to allow DMU to pass	5	09:25	09:25	09:25	09:25	09:25	09:25
Bratton Fleming	15	09:40	11:40	13:40	15:40	17:40	19:40
passing halt to allow steamers to cross	5	09:45	09:45	09:45	09:45	09:45	09:45
Blackmoor	18	10:03	12:03	14:03	16:03	18:03	20:03
Parracombe Halt	13	10:16	12:16	14:16	16:16	18:16	20:16
Woody Bay	9	10:25	12:25	14:25	16:25	18:25	20:25
Caffyn's Halt	9	10:34	12:34	14:34	16:34	18:34	20:34
Lynton - arrival	6	10:40	12:40	14:40	16:40	18:40	20:40
wait (coal and water) - departure at	20	10:45	12:45	14:45	16:45	18:45	parked
	120						

Lynton - Barnstaple Town: a recreation from the historic timetable of the narrow-gauge steam railway

Two further factors are significant: the Lynton Station is atop a very steep hill about a mile from and over 200 feet above the town; the road between has no footpath and (the author observed) some drivers certainly drive in great haste; it is not, therefore, appealing to a Lynton pedestrian. Neither is there any scope at the station site for car parking, and this is a necessary requirement in today's times.

It would suggest that an alternative Lynton terminus would find favour. One option is to establish an alternative site a little further down the line, one offering parking. The Woody Bay station site would seem suitable, but having arrived there from Lynton by car it begs the question: why not simply carry on by car to Barnstaple?

A second and more intriguing possibility would be to extend the railway line **north** from the former Lynton station along the 700ft / 220m contour line in a sweeping curve to the left (north and west) to arrive at a point on Lydiate Lane which offers space for a new station *and* parking. Such a line would sit just above those existing houses built just below that same contour line and just north of it- *see map*.

A bus service from Lynmouth (and through Lynton) to a new station site would also contribute to either location.

In contemplating the essential purpose of restoring 'lost' lines, the narrow-gauge character of the Lynton-Barnstaple railway might be considered as an impediment; certainly so, were the people of Lynton and Lynmouth to aspire to a modern, comfortable, frequent and (relatively) speedy service with which they might commute to Barnstaple.

The proprietors of today's short section of the line have admirable hopes, intentions and plans to restore more of it; however, therein is a conflict of sorts: even the railway's greatest proponents would shirk from claiming it to be a desirable offering for commuters.

Of course, the Lynton *steam* railway is *not* a viable train for commuters. The residents of Lynton most likely would welcome a 'proper' commuter train, one that travels faster than the steam train; certainly so for frequent and periodical travel: for that a DMU would be required.

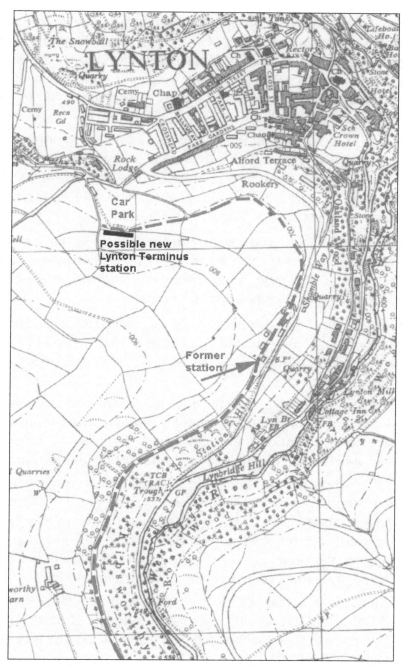

Possible location for new Lynton station and car park

This is the one significant factor which merits the most considerate evaluation: the group of enthusiasts have long sought (and succeeded to a promising degree) to keep the railway 'alive', to restore it to its former status; and a significant extension to its present short length is within reach; however, it remains a long way to go to reach Barnstaple once again.

In terms of tourism promotion, the narrow-gauge steamers of the heritage railway are very attractive to tourists, and an economic benefit to the town of Lynton/Lynmouth, no doubt (they attract 40,000 train rides each year on a track which is only about one mile in length), but they are *not* commuter trains. What can be done?

Assuming that Lynton and Lynmouth expressed a desire for a commuter train, a DMU, then what solution resolves the resultant incompatibility of the line: slow, infrequent, narrow-gauge rail or modern, frequent and speedy standard-gauge?

It seems reasonable; indeed, only fair, that the interests (and passionate enthusiasms) of the incumbent narrow-gauge railway promoters should be protected, as far as it is possible to do so. There are several answers:

(1) The narrow-gauge railway could convert to standard gauge (a complete change of rolling stock would be needed). The benefit would be a fully restored and operational railway line the length of the original railway and at no cost to the incumbent owners of the existing line; or

(2) The whole of the line could be built as three-rail, enabling concurrent operation of standard- and narrow-gauge trains. The narrow-gauge railway owners might, reasonably, have to pay for the additional, third rail; but that is relatively inexpensive in comparison with paying for the remainder of the whole line to be laid as narrow-gauge; and so, this would seem to offer an attractive solution.

Of course, the narrow-gauge 'steamers' would be far slower than a modern DMU, and this would necessitate a number of passing places ("loops") on the line to allow the steamer to shift out of the way of the passing or oncoming DMU.

Horrabridge station with 3-rail track in the days when the GWR operated 'broad' (7 feet) gauge and also with the LSWR standard 4ft 8.5 inch gauge - both ran on the same (three rails) railway track.

The 'line-sharing", concurrent operation is feasible; such exists elsewhere in the world; indeed, it existed in Devon in days long gone by; it is therefore proposed and illustrated in the following timetables, one each for the 'steamer' service and the DMU commuter service.

The Lynton narrow-gauge railway was also built in a manner suited to narrow-gauge trains, with tighter curves, for example, and a relatively steep gradient; as such, the most careful and creative of modifications would be necessary were it to be restored all along its length as suitable for a standard-gauge railway (with a third rail for the steamer).

The DMU timetable is a construction of what would be required in terms of speed as a minimum, were the service to appeal to commuters; it suggests a travel time of 46 minutes (24 mph) between Lynton Station and a new Barnstaple Town platform.

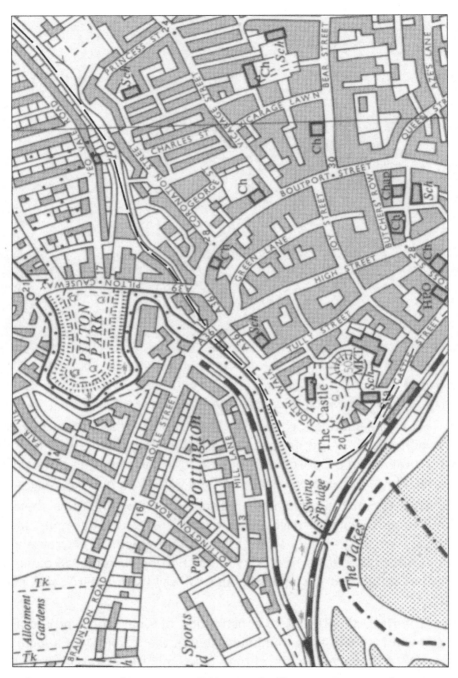

*Convergence of **Lynton** and **Ilfracombe** lines at Barnstaple Town*

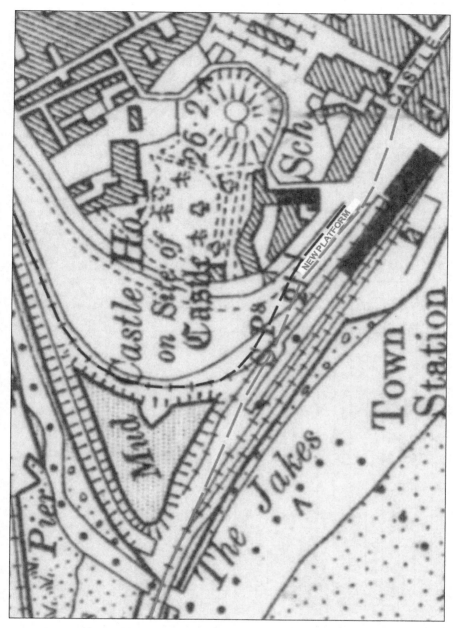

New Barnstaple Town platform for Lynton and Ilfracombe lines

2b - DMU

THE LYNTON FLYER (DMU)	minutes	20.7	miles	24 mph	1 train	02:00	cycle
	en route	08:00	10:00	12:00	14:00	16:00	18:00
Lynton - departure		08:00	10:00	12:00	14:00	16:00	18:00
Caffyn's Halt	5	08:05	10:05	12:05	14:05	16:05	18:05
Woody Bay	5	08:10	10:10	12:10	14:10	16:10	18:10
Parracombe Halt	5	08:15	10:15	12:15	14:15	16:15	18:15
Blackmoor	6	08:21	10:21	12:21	14:21	16:21	18:21
Bratton Fleming	7	08:28	10:28	12:28	14:28	16:28	18:28
Chelfham	7	08:35	10:35	12:35	14:35	16:35	18:35
Snapper Halt	5	08:40	10:40	12:40	14:40	16:40	18:40
Barnstaple Town	6	08:46	10:46	12:46	14:46	16:46	18:46
Barnstaple river bridge LINK - see schema	5	08:51	10:51	12:51	14:51	16:51	18:51
reverse	2	08:53	10:53	12:53	14:53	16:53	18:53
Barnstaple Junction - arrival	5	08:58	10:58	12:58	14:58	16:58	18:58
wait - before departure at	2	09:00	11:00	13:00	15:00	17:00	19:00
Barnstaple river bridge LINK - see schema	5	09:05	11:05	13:05	15:05	17:05	19:05
reverse	2	09:07	11:07	13:07	15:07	17:07	19:07
Barnstaple Town	5	09:12	11:12	13:12	15:12	17:12	19:12
Snapper Halt	6	09:18	11:18	13:18	15:18	17:18	19:18
Chelfham	5	09:23	11:23	13:23	15:23	17:23	19:23
Bratton Fleming	7	09:30	11:30	13:30	15:30	17:30	19:30
Blackmoor	7	09:37	11:37	13:37	15:37	17:37	19:37
Parracombe Halt	6	09:43	11:43	13:43	15:43	17:43	19:43
Woody Bay	5	09:48	11:48	13:48	15:48	17:48	19:48
Caffyn's Halt	5	09:53	11:53	13:53	15:53	17:53	19:53
Lynton - arrival	5	09:58	11:58	13:58	15:58	17:58	19:58
wait - before departure at	2	10:00	12:00	14:00	16:00	18:00	parked
	120						

Lynton - Barnstaple Town: a postulated timetable for a modern DMU service

The Devon and Somerset Railway: Taunton to Barnstaple

On the assumption that some of the 'lost' lines would be restored before others, the former Devon and Somerset Railway (Barnstaple - Taunton) is shown as two halves: Barnstaple to Dulverton (almost exactly half-way and also the terminus for the line from Tiverton) and Dulverton to Taunton.

Just one modern DMU train could operate each half of the former line, offering departures at two-hour intervals (which, it is thought, would be the least that any service would have to offer).

They are relatively long branch lines and hence the distance militates against a higher frequency of service (bearing in mind too the cost of rolling stock, its operational cost, and the likely number of passengers on a very rural line).

Ultimately it would make sense to operate the two halves as one line with a DMU starting each morning at each end of the line. The following timetables model both options.

However, restoration of the line at the Barnstaple end presents a number of challenges, including:

- the track-bed within the town limits of the town from the historic Victoria Road station to Portmore roundabout has been overlaid with a new road,

- from Portmore roundabout on the A361 North Devon Link Road to Borner's Bridge roundabout (which is north of South Molton), the track-bed has also been subsumed by that most important road connecting North Devon with the M5 motorway near Tiverton, the 'Link Road'.

It's nigh on exactly 10 miles between Portmore roundabout and Borner's Bridge roundabout. The historic route of the railway diverged from the modern A361 at that point, the railway on a more northerly route heading east.

A great deal of work is currently underway (at the time of writing in late 2022) to enhance the A361 "Link Road" on that stretch, including the addition of a third (overtaking) lane along approximately half of it.

The contact is worth **£46,560,558** and was awarded to Alan Griffiths Contractors of Abergavenny. The Transport Secretary, Grant Shapps, described the funding as *"a clear indication of our commitment to levelling up and investing in transport infrastructure"*.

The cost of, broadly, £9 million per mile for an extra road lane (plus a new roundabout and other improvements) is considerably more than the cost of laying new railway track on existing track-bed; however, it may be an indication of the likely cost per mile for any 'virgin' sections of railway that might be required in a network restoration. Several relatively short sections of such are postulated within this paper.

What is interesting to speculate, in the context of railway restoration, is that it would seem feasible to recreate the 10 miles of railway from Portmore to Borner's Bridge *alongside* the North Devon Link Road.

Of course the Filleigh Viaduct represents one element which mandates a solution in the event of such an approach; railways work best on the flat and level; they do not cope with slopes (metal wheels on metal rails slip); hence, the original construction of the viaduct. It would seem that a restored railway line would necessitate the use of that viaduct. It presently carries two vehicle lanes. Vehicular traffic could be halted by traffic lights for the approximately two minutes required for the train to traverse the viaduct and slip left/right to the new rail track parallel with the road. The weight of the train would likely dictate that it crossed in the centre of the viaduct (as it did historically) and monopolised *both* traffic lanes.

Within Barnstaple from the Taw Bridge to Portmore, the railway would run on the old track-bed until it crossed the car parking area for the 'Retail Park', and thence it would run parallel with the road and across the A39/A361 junction roundabout, traffic lights being required to safeguard its crossing.

Level crossings would also be required along the Link Road where minor roads join. The low frequency of the trains suggest that the disruption to traffic on such (relatively little used) roads would be very minimal.

Such crossings as this are unlikely to re-emerge into service exactly as they once were - unattended and without a gate or traffic lights. Historically, they served on 'Light Railways' which enjoyed a much more lax safety standard than would be permitted today (and also much lower speed limits as a consequence - in some instances the train was obliged to stop completely before proceeding). Hence, in a restoration scenario every crossing would have to be safeguarded by traffic lights as a bare minimum, but they would not be manned by (expensive) personnel.

Automatically-operated gates are also perfectly feasible for the more busy crossings, with modern-day automation tools. Photo: Bernard Mills.

STAGE ONE   3

The BARUM LINK	minutes		miles	25 mph	1 train	02:00	cycle
	en route	08:00	10:00	12:00	14:00	16:00	18:00
Barnstaple Junction - departure		08:00	10:00	12:00	14:00	16:00	18:00
Swimbridge	10	08:10	10:10	12:10	14:10	16:10	18:10
Filleigh	7	08:17	10:17	12:17	14:17	16:17	18:17
South Molton	9	08:26	10:26	12:26	14:26	16:26	18:26
Bishops Nympton	10	08:36	10:36	12:36	14:36	16:36	18:36
Yeo Mill Halt	6	08:42	10:42	12:42	14:42	16:42	18:42
East Anstey	6	08:48	10:48	12:48	14:48	16:48	18:48
Dulverton - arrival	10	08:58	10:58	12:58	14:58	16:58	18:58
wait - before departure at	2	09:00	11:00	13:00	15:00	17:00	19:00
East Anstey	10	09:10	11:10	13:10	15:10	17:10	19:10
Yeo Mill Halt	6	09:16	11:16	13:16	15:16	17:16	19:16
Bishops Nympton	6	09:22	11:22	13:22	15:22	17:22	19:22
South Molton	10	09:32	11:32	13:32	15:32	17:32	19:32
Filleigh	9	09:41	11:41	13:41	15:41	17:41	19:41
Swimbridge	7	09:48	11:48	13:48	15:48	17:48	19:48
Barnstaple Junction - arrival	10	09:58	11:58	13:58	15:58	17:58	19:58
wait - before departure at	2	10:00	12:00	14:00	16:00	18:00	parked
	120						

Barnstaple to Dulverton: a recreation from the historic timetable

STAGE ONE 4

The EXMOOR RANGER	minutes		miles	25 mph	1 train	02:00	cycle
	en route	08:00	10:00	12:00	14:00	16:00	18:00
Taunton - departure		08:00	10:00	12:00	14:00	16:00	18:00
Norton Fitzwarren	5	08:05	10:05	12:05	14:05	16:05	18:05
Milverton	10	08:15	10:15	12:15	14:15	16:15	18:15
Wiveliscombe	9	08:24	10:24	12:24	14:24	16:24	18:24
Venn Cross	11	08:35	10:35	12:35	14:35	16:35	18:35
Morebath	7	08:42	10:42	12:42	14:42	16:42	18:42
Morebath Jcn.	5	08:47	10:47	12:47	14:47	16:47	18:47
Dulverton - arrival	6	08:53	10:53	12:53	14:53	16:53	18:53
wait - before departure at	7	09:00	11:00	13:00	15:00	17:00	19:00
Morebath Junction Halt	6	09:06	11:06	13:06	15:06	17:06	19:06
Morebath	5	09:11	11:11	13:11	15:11	17:11	19:11
Venn Cross	7	09:18	11:18	13:18	15:18	17:18	19:18
Wiveliscombe	11	09:29	11:29	13:29	15:29	17:29	19:29
Milverton	9	09:38	11:38	13:38	15:38	17:38	19:38
Norton Fitzwarren	10	09:48	11:48	13:48	15:48	17:48	19:48
Taunton - arrival	5	09:53	11:53	13:53	15:53	17:53	19:53
wait - before departure at	7	10:00	12:00	14:00	16:00	18:00	*parked*
	120						

Taunton to Dulverton: a recreation from the historic timetable

STAGE TWO 3 (and 4) combined

The EXMOOR RANGER (eastbound)	minutes	49	miles	25 mph 2 trains		02:00	interval
Barnstaple Junction - departure	en route	08:00	10:00	12:00	14:00	16:00	18:00
Swimbridge	10	08:10	10:10	12:10	14:10	16:10	18:10
Filleigh	7	08:17	10:17	12:17	14:17	16:17	18:17
South Molton	9	08:26	10:26	12:26	14:26	16:26	18:26
Bishops Nympton	10	08:36	10:36	12:36	14:36	16:36	18:36
Yeo Mill Halt	6	08:42	10:42	12:42	14:42	16:42	18:42
East Anstey	6	08:48	10:48	12:48	14:48	16:48	18:48
Dulverton - arrival	10	08:58	10:58	12:58	14:58	16:58	18:58
the passing place where east meets west	eastbound train arrives, westbound train waiting for it						
wait - before departure at	5	09:03	11:03	13:03	15:03	17:03	19:03
Morebath Junction Halt	6	09:09	11:09	13:09	15:09	17:09	19:09
Morebath	5	09:14	11:14	13:14	15:14	17:14	19:14
Venn Cross	7	09:21	11:21	13:21	15:21	17:21	19:21
Wiveliscombe	11	09:32	11:32	13:32	15:32	17:32	19:32
Milverton	9	09:41	11:41	13:41	15:41	17:41	19:41
Norton Fitzwarren	10	09:51	11:51	13:51	15:51	17:51	19:51
Taunton - arrival	5	09:56	11:56	13:56	15:56	17:56	19:56
wait - before departure at	4	10:00	12:00	14:00	16:00	18:00	parked
	120						

The two lines are merged, eastbound trains run from end to end.
Barnstaple to Taunton: a recreation from the historic timetable

The EXMOOR RANGER (westbound)	minutes	49	miles	25 mph	2 trains	02:00	interval
	en route	08:00	10:00	12:00	14:00	16:00	18:00
Taunton - departure		08:00	10:00	12:00	14:00	16:00	18:00
Norton Fitzwarren	5	08:05	10:05	12:05	14:05	16:05	18:05
Milverton	10	08:15	10:15	12:15	14:15	16:15	18:15
Wiveliscombe	9	08:24	10:24	12:24	14:24	16:24	18:24
Venn Cross	11	08:35	10:35	12:35	14:35	16:35	18:35
Morebath	7	08:42	10:42	12:42	14:42	16:42	18:42
Morebath Jcn.	5	08:47	10:47	12:47	14:47	16:47	18:47
Dulverton - arrival	6	08:53	10:53	12:53	14:53	16:53	18:53
the passing place where east meets west			westbound train awaits arrival of the eastbound train				
wait - before departure at	5	08:58	10:58	12:58	14:58	16:58	18:58
East Anstey	10	09:08	11:08	13:08	15:08	17:08	19:08
Yeo Mill Halt	6	09:14	11:14	13:14	15:14	17:14	19:14
Bishops Nympton	6	09:20	11:20	13:20	15:20	17:20	19:20
South Molton	10	09:30	11:30	13:30	15:30	17:30	19:30
Filleigh	9	09:39	11:39	13:39	15:39	17:39	19:39
Swimbridge	7	09:46	11:46	13:46	15:46	17:46	19:46
Barnstaple Junction - arrival	10	09:56	11:56	13:56	15:56	17:56	19:56
wait - before departure at	4	10:00	12:00	14:00	16:00	18:00	parked
	120						

The westbound service.
Taunton to Barnstaple: a recreation from the historic timetable

The Exe Valley Railway

The existing **Tiverton Parkway** station (formerly the Sampford Peverell Halt until 1986) has no branch line connections at all. Access to it can only be gained by car. In fact, due to the extensive geographical area that the station serves in enabling access to the railway main line, cars travel from very far afield to use the station, and a great expanse of car parking areas into hitherto-before fields has proliferated. This in itself vouches for a widespread need to access the railway.

The historical decision to abandon the then existing Tiverton *Junction* station which was 1.6 miles (2,600 metres) south of *Parkway* (and which did actually provide for an onward rail connection to Tiverton town: the Tiverton Branch line - *more on that below*) was founded on the principle of abandonment of branch lines in favour of the car; and, of course, Parkway is in close proximity to the M5 Junction 27, to the A361 North Devon Link Road (west) and the A38 (east).

The extensive and expanding swathes of car parking areas at Tiverton Parkway evidence the widespread, far-reaching geographical 'hinterland' served by the station. From personal experience, the author can attest to the fact that this hinterland extends west as far as Hartland in Torridge District, a distance of 58 miles.

This would suggest that restored branch lines, connecting to the mainline, would seem likely to be well-patronised. This paper proposes such restored connections to connect to the main line in the form of a restored Barnstaple - Taunton line across Exmoor, a restored Tiverton Junction connecting Tiverton town, and a restored connection at Stoke Canon on the Exe Valley line; it also proposes reconnections at Bere Alston (for Tavistock), at Bodmin Parkway (for Bodmin and Padstow) and at Marsh Mills (for Tavistock to Plymouth).

For the moment, we will return to the Exe Valley. Three lines were originally built: Tiverton Junction to Tiverton town in 1848, Tiverton town to Dulverton in 1884 (connecting with the Taunton to Barnstaple line) and Tiverton to Stoke Canon in 1885.

Adhering to the aspirations for service frequencies being 'reasonable' i.e. no more than 2 hour intervals *and ideally more frequent*, the restored services are proposed **as two**:

The first would run between a restored connection at Tiverton Junction to Tiverton town and thence on to Dulverton, with a frequency of one train every 90 minutes at all points on the line;

The second service would run from Tiverton (town) to Stoke Canon, to a restored (Stoke Canon) platform on the *western* side of the mainline - *see map* - where it would be possible to join or alight from a mainline train for the onwards journey. The service frequency is 75 minutes.

As an alternative to the second service, the third timetable is for a train which continues on *from* Stoke Canon to Exeter St. Davids and on to Exeter Central. The service frequency, because of the greater distance, widens to one and three-quarter hours.

Reinstatement of the lines through Tiverton, the one to Stoke Canon particularly, would represent a challenge because of the potential for conflict with the car on the Tiverton 'south bypass'. A new platform would be sited very close to the historic station (demolished) site - *see map*.

For much of the length of the bypass road there is sufficient 'width' of land upon which to restore the railway line.

The train would function akin to a tram on those parts of the bypass road on which it encroached, crossing several traffic roundabouts (marked as orange dots on the historic map) until it reached its original track-bed to the south west of the town. In doing so it would also share a bridge over the River Exe, all such interrelating of train and car controlled by traffic lights.

The TIVVY BUMPER

	minutes	30.5	miles	cycle	1 train	01:30	cycle	inc. Tiverton Junction		20mph
Tiverton (town) - departure	en route	08:00	09:30	11:00	12:30	14:00	15:30	17:00	18:30	20:00	20:30
Halberton Halt	7	08:07	09:37	11:07	12:37	14:07	15:37	17:07	18:37	20:07	20:37
Tiverton Junction	6	08:13	09:43	11:13	12:43	14:13	15:43	17:13	18:43	20:13	20:43
wait - before departure at	2	08:15	09:45	11:15	12:45	14:15	15:45	17:15	18:45	20:15	20:45
Halberton Halt	6	08:21	09:51	11:21	12:51	14:21	15:51	17:21	18:51	20:21	20:51
Tiverton (town) - arrival	7	08:28	09:58	11:28	12:58	14:28	15:58	17:28	18:58	20:28	20:58
wait - before departure at	2	08:30	10:00	11:30	13:00	14:30	16:00	17:30	19:00	20:30	parked
Bolham Halt	5	08:35	10:05	11:35	13:05	14:35	16:05	17:35	19:05		
Cove Halt	8	08:43	10:13	11:43	13:13	14:43	16:13	17:43	19:13		
Bampton	5	08:48	10:18	11:48	13:18	14:48	16:18	17:48	19:18		
Morebath Junction	5	08:53	10:23	11:53	13:23	14:53	16:23	17:53	19:23		
Dulverton - arrival	5	08:58	10:28	11:58	13:28	14:58	16:28	17:58	19:28		
wait - before departure at	2	09:00	10:30	12:00	13:30	15:00	16:30	18:00	19:30		
Morebath Junction	5	09:05	10:35	12:05	13:35	15:05	16:35	18:05	19:35		
Bampton	5	09:10	10:40	12:10	13:40	15:10	16:40	18:10	19:40		
Cove Halt	5	09:15	10:45	12:15	13:45	15:15	16:45	18:15	19:45		
Bolham Halt	8	09:23	10:53	12:23	13:53	15:23	16:53	18:23	19:53		
Tiverton (town) - arrival	5	09:28	10:58	12:28	13:58	15:28	16:58	18:28	19:58		
wait - before departure at	2	09:30	11:00	12:30	14:00	15:30	17:00	18:30	20:00		
	90										

Tiverton (town) - Tiverton (mainline) Junction - Dulverton:
a recreation from the historic timetable

6a train terminates at main line junction

The EXE VALLEY EXPLORER	minutes en route	10.75 miles one way	1 train	01:15	cycle	17 mph				
Tiverton (town) - departure	6	08:00	09:15	10:30	11:45	13:00	14:15	15:30	16:45	18:00	19:15
West Exe Halt	8	08:06	09:21	10:36	11:51	13:06	14:21	15:36	16:51	18:06	19:21
Cadeleigh	3	08:14	09:29	10:44	11:59	13:14	14:29	15:44	16:59	18:14	19:29
Burn Halt	5	08:17	09:32	10:47	12:02	13:17	14:32	15:47	17:02	18:17	19:32
Up Exe Halt	3	08:22	09:37	10:52	12:07	13:22	14:37	15:52	17:07	18:22	19:37
Thorverton	5	08:25	09:40	10:55	12:10	13:25	14:40	15:55	17:10	18:25	19:40
Brampford Speke	4	08:30	09:45	11:00	12:15	13:30	14:45	16:00	17:15	18:30	19:45
Stoke Canon - arrival - join main line train	3	08:34	09:49	11:04	12:19	13:34	14:49	16:04	17:19	18:34	19:49
wait - before departure at		08:37	09:52	11:07	12:22	13:37	14:52	16:07	17:22	18:37	19:52
Brampford Speke	4	08:41	09:56	11:11	12:26	13:41	14:56	16:11	17:26	18:41	19:56
Thorverton	5	08:46	10:01	11:16	12:31	13:46	15:01	16:16	17:31	18:46	20:01
Up Exe Halt	3	08:49	10:04	11:19	12:34	13:49	15:04	16:19	17:34	18:49	20:04
Burn Halt	5	08:54	10:09	11:24	12:39	13:54	15:09	16:24	17:39	18:54	20:09
Cadeleigh	3	08:57	10:12	11:27	12:42	13:57	15:12	16:27	17:42	18:57	20:12
West Exe Halt	8	09:05	10:20	11:35	12:50	14:05	15:20	16:35	17:50	19:05	20:20
Tiverton (town) - arrival	6	09:11	10:26	11:41	12:56	14:11	15:26	16:41	17:56	19:11	20:26
wait - before departure at	75	09:15	10:30	11:45	13:00	14:15	15:30	16:45	18:00	19:15	parked

Tiverton - Stoke Canon (mainline junction):
a recreation from the historic timetable

The EXE VALLEY EXPLORER	minutes	10.75	miles one way		1 train	01:45	cycle	17 mph	
	en route	08:00	09:45	11:30	13:15	15:00	16:45	18:30	20:15
Tiverton (town) - departure		08:00	09:45	11:30	13:15	15:00	16:45	18:30	20:15
West Exe Halt	6	08:06	09:51	11:36	13:21	15:06	16:51	18:36	20:21
Cadeleigh	8	08:14	09:59	11:44	13:29	15:14	16:59	18:44	20:29
Burn Halt	3	08:17	10:02	11:47	13:32	15:17	17:02	18:47	20:32
Up Exe Halt	5	08:22	10:07	11:52	13:37	15:22	17:07	18:52	20:37
Thorverton	3	08:25	10:10	11:55	13:40	15:25	17:10	18:55	20:40
Brampford Speke	5	08:30	10:15	12:00	13:45	15:30	17:15	19:00	20:45
Stoke Canon	4	08:34	10:19	12:04	13:49	15:34	17:19	19:04	20:49
Exeter St. David's	6	08:40	10:25	12:10	13:55	15:40	17:25	19:10	20:55
Exeter Central	7	08:47	10:32	12:17	14:02	15:47	17:32	19:17	21:02
wait - before departure at	3	08:50	10:35	12:20	14:05	15:50	17:35	19:20	21:05
Exeter St. David's	7	08:57	10:42	12:27	14:12	15:57	17:42	19:27	21:12
wait - before departure at	3	09:00	10:45	12:30	14:15	16:00	17:45	19:30	21:15
Stoke Canon	6	09:06	10:51	12:36	14:21	16:06	17:51	19:36	21:21
Brampford Speke	4	09:10	10:55	12:40	14:25	16:10	17:55	19:40	21:25
Thorverton	5	09:15	11:00	12:45	14:30	16:15	18:00	19:45	21:30
Up Exe Halt	3	09:18	11:03	12:48	14:33	16:18	18:03	19:48	21:33
Burn Halt	5	09:23	11:08	12:53	14:38	16:23	18:08	19:53	21:38
Cadeleigh	3	09:26	11:11	12:56	14:41	16:26	18:11	19:56	21:41
West Exe Halt	8	09:34	11:19	13:04	14:49	16:34	18:19	20:04	21:49
Tiverton (town) - arrival	6	09:40	11:25	13:10	14:55	16:40	18:25	20:10	21:55
wait - before departure at	5	09:45	11:30	13:15	15:00	16:45	18:30	20:15	*parked*
	105								

Tiverton - Stoke Canon and Exeter:
a recreation from the historic timetable

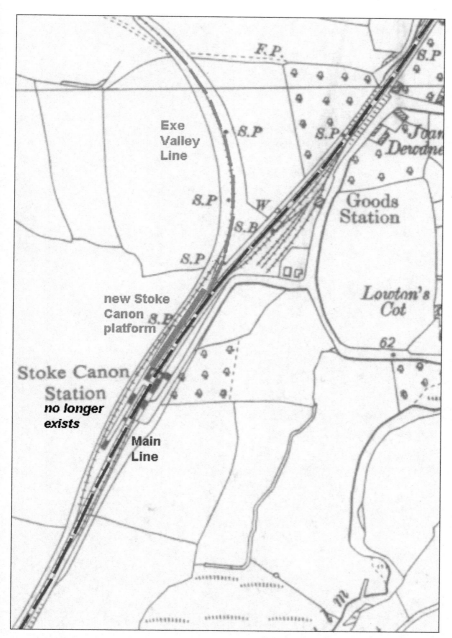

A new platform for the junction of the Exe Valley and main lines, slightly to the north of the old (non-existent now) station

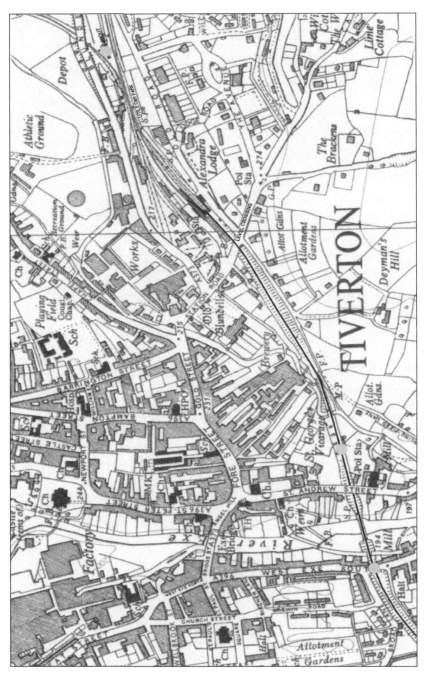

Tiverton: restored railway, south of town centre

Halwill Junction: key junction for northern Devon and north Cornwall.

Four lines come together from the north, from: Launceston, Bude and Torrington; the Torrington line to Okehampton is to the south.

The location of a new station location is north of the village. No appropriation or demolition of houses in Beeching Close would be necessary.

The line of the proposed restored railway line sweeps wide of the village and the former station site in a wide arc to rejoin the original track-bed just south of all houses - the line to Okehampton and the Exeter connection. Consequently, <u>there would be no disruption to the village</u>, save for two new level crossings being required *(see plans)*.

The map illustrates just one example of how it should be entirely feasible in most instances to bypass developments impacting / impeding original (historic) railway lines and achieve a contiguous route for restored railway lines.

The first (east) line from the north is from Torrington; that line is a continuation of the line from Barnstaple Junction to Bideford and thence Torrington.

The second (central) line is to/from Bude via Holsworthy.

The third line is to/from Launceston, from where it continues to Wadebridge and ultimately connects to Padstow.

Note that all three of these lines would be physically separate - i.e. no track sharing all the way to the new station (again, adhering to the simplicity and safety aspirations of single line working).

To the south, the (Torrington) line goes on towards Okehampton for onward connections to the existing operational line to Exeter and a potentially restored line south to Tavistock.

Halwill Junction would be a prime candidate for a locomotive and rolling stock maintenance depot, having relatively little development (and none need be disrupted) with fields abounding for a spur track to such a maintenance facility. As such it would generate employment and prosperity for the village. The train connection would be valuable too.

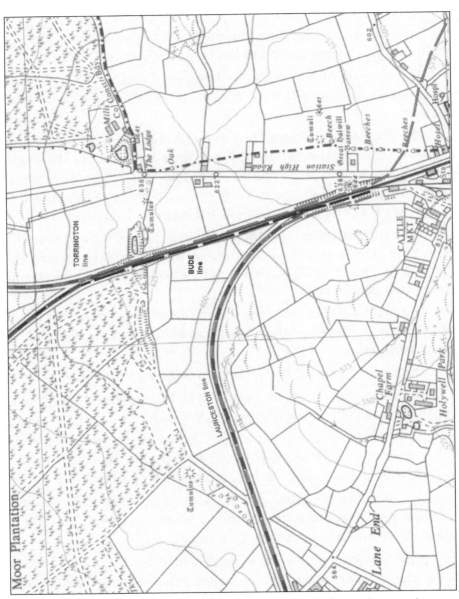

Halwill Junction: three lines approach from the north.
A new station is located north of Beeching Close

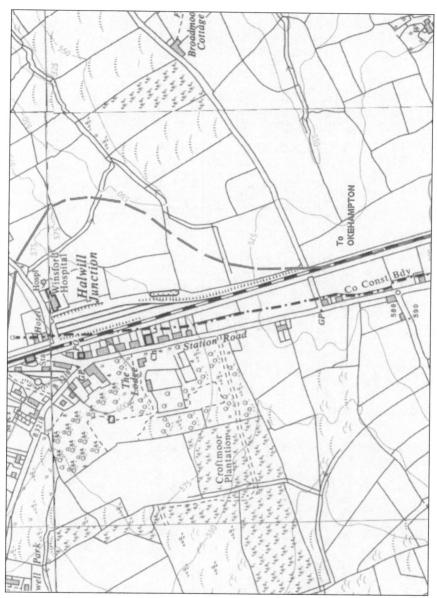

Halwill Junction: the Okehampton 'through' line to the south, a diversion from the original, bypasses the village.

The TORRIDGE RIVER	minutes	14.3 miles one way	1 train	01:15	cycle 26 mph					
Barnstaple Junction - departure	en route	08:00	09:15	10:30	11:45	13:00	14:15	15:30	16:45	18:00	19:15
Fremington	6	08:06	09:21	10:36	11:51	13:06	14:21	15:36	16:51	18:06	19:21
Instow	8	08:14	09:29	10:44	11:59	13:14	14:29	15:44	16:59	18:14	19:29
Bideford	8	08:22	09:37	10:52	12:07	13:22	14:37	15:52	17:07	18:22	19:37
Torrington - arrival	13	08:35	09:50	11:05	12:20	13:35	14:50	16:05	17:20	18:35	19:50
wait - before departure at	2	08:37	09:52	11:07	12:22	13:37	14:52	16:07	17:22	18:37	19:52
Bideford	13	08:50	10:05	11:20	12:35	13:50	15:05	16:20	17:35	18:50	20:05
Instow	8	08:58	10:13	11:28	12:43	13:58	15:13	16:28	17:43	18:58	20:13
Fremington	8	09:06	10:21	11:36	12:51	14:06	15:21	16:36	17:51	19:06	20:21
Barnstaple Junction - arrival	6	09:12	10:27	11:42	12:57	14:12	15:27	16:42	17:57	19:12	20:27
wait - before departure at	3	09:15	10:30	11:45	13:00	14:15	15:30	16:45	18:00	19:15	parked
	75										

Barnstaple Junction to Torrington: a recreation from the historic timetable

8								
The OLDE CLAY	*minutes*	20.75	miles one way	**1 train**	*22 mph*	02:00	cycle
Torrington - *departure*	*en route*	**08:00**	**10:00**	**12:00**	**14:00**	**16:00**	**18:00**	**20:00**
Watergate Halt	5	08:05	10:05	12:05	14:05	16:05	18:05	20:05
Yarde Halt	9	08:14	10:14	12:14	14:14	16:14	18:14	20:14
Dunsbear Halt	4	08:18	10:18	12:18	14:18	16:18	18:18	20:18
Petrockstow	7	08:25	10:25	12:25	14:25	16:25	18:25	20:25
Meeth Halt	7	08:32	10:32	12:32	14:32	16:32	18:32	20:32
Hatherleigh	7	08:39	10:39	12:39	14:39	16:39	18:39	20:39
Hole	12	08:51	10:51	12:51	14:51	16:51	18:51	20:51
Halwill Junction - ***arrival***	6	08:57	10:57	12:57	14:57	16:57	18:57	20:57
*wait - before **departure** at*	3	**09:00**	**11:00**	**13:00**	**15:00**	**17:00**	**19:00**	**21:00**
Hole	6	09:06	11:06	13:06	15:06	17:06	19:06	21:06
Hatherleigh	12	09:18	11:18	13:18	15:18	17:18	19:18	21:18
Meeth Halt	7	09:25	11:25	13:25	15:25	17:25	19:25	21:25
Petrockstow	7	09:32	11:32	13:32	15:32	17:32	19:32	21:32
Dunsbear Halt	7	09:39	11:39	13:39	15:39	17:39	19:39	21:39
Yarde Halt	4	09:43	11:43	13:43	15:43	17:43	19:43	21:43
Watergate Halt	9	09:52	11:52	13:52	15:52	17:52	19:52	21:52
Torrington - ***arrival***	5	09:57	11:57	13:57	15:57	17:57	19:57	21:57
*wait - before **departure** at*	3	**10:00**	**12:00**	**14:00**	**16:00**	**18:00**	**20:00**	*parked*
	120							

Torrington to Halwill Junction: a recreation from the historic timetable

Halwill Junction to Bude.

A Bude station would need to be relocated a little way from its historic location - *see map*. However, that particular location offers the considerable advantage of an undeveloped site for a car park adjacent to the station.

Bude and its beaches to the surf are a mecca for surfers; the town also enjoys a significant number of Victorian-era guest houses, all of whom would probably welcome a restored rail connection bringing tourists. The golf club, too, would welcome golfers arriving by train from all across the region on an hourly service from the restored hub of Halwill Junction.

Such a restored service would also transit the town of Holsworthy along the way; fortunately, it benefits from the two preserved viaducts east and west of the town. One new bridge over the road *immediately west* of the Waitrose supermarket would require to be built, and the track-bed would also transit the south edge of the supermarket car park. In a time when the budget supermarkets are gaining market share, the Waitrose organisation might conceivably welcome the new customers that such an immediate connection would surely deliver.

9

The SURF

	minutes	18.5	miles one way	1 train			cycle	24 mph		
	en route									
Bude - departure	10	08:00	09:30	11:00	12:30	14:00	15:30	17:00	18:30	20:00
Whitstone	10	08:10	09:40	11:10	12:40	14:10	15:40	17:10	18:40	20:10
Holsworthy	10	08:20	09:50	11:20	12:50	14:20	15:50	17:20	18:50	20:20
Dunsland Cross	10	08:30	10:00	11:30	13:00	14:30	16:00	17:30	19:00	20:30
Halwill Junction - arrival	7	08:37	10:07	11:37	13:07	14:37	16:07	17:37	19:07	20:37
wait - before departure at	8	08:45	10:15	11:45	13:15	14:45	16:15	17:45	19:15	20:45
Dunsland Cross	7	08:52	10:22	11:52	13:22	14:52	16:22	17:52	19:22	20:52
Holsworthy	10	09:02	10:32	12:02	13:32	15:02	16:32	18:02	19:32	21:02
Whitstone	10	09:12	10:42	12:12	13:42	15:12	16:42	18:12	19:42	21:12
Bude - arrival	10	09:22	10:52	12:22	13:52	15:22	16:52	18:22	19:52	21:22
wait - before departure at	8	09:30	11:00	12:30	14:00	15:30	17:00	18:30	20:00	parked
	90									

Bude to Halwill Junction: a recreation from the historic timetable

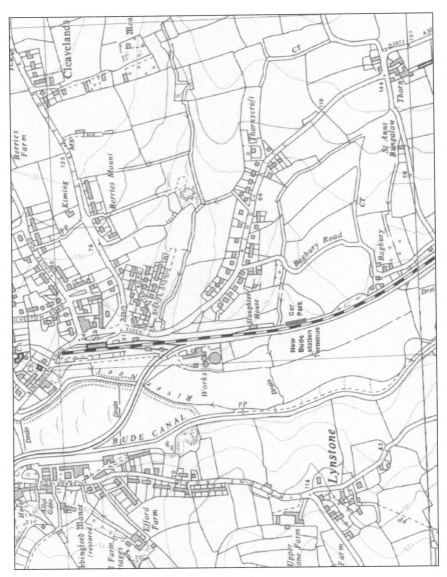

Bude: a new station (platform) south of the original one.
The location also offers scope for a car park.

10

The LAUNCESTON LIMITED

	minutes	14.7 miles one way		1 train	01:00 cycle	30 mph						
	en route	08:00	09:00	10:00	11:00	12:00	13:00	14:00	15:00	16:00	17:00	18:00	19:00
Halwill Junction - departure		08:00	09:00	10:00	11:00	12:00	13:00	14:00	15:00	16:00	17:00	18:00	19:00
Ashwater	10	08:10	09:10	10:10	11:10	12:10	13:10	14:10	15:10	16:10	17:10	18:10	19:10
Tower Hill	7	08:17	09:17	10:17	11:17	12:17	13:17	14:17	15:17	16:17	17:17	18:17	19:17
Launceston - arrival	9	08:26	09:26	10:26	11:26	12:26	13:26	14:26	15:26	16:26	17:26	18:26	19:26
wait - before departure at	4	08:30	09:30	10:30	11:30	12:30	13:30	14:30	15:30	16:30	17:30	18:30	19:30
Tower Hill	9	08:39	09:39	10:39	11:39	12:39	13:39	14:39	15:39	16:39	17:39	18:39	19:39
Ashwater	7	08:46	09:46	10:46	11:46	12:46	13:46	14:46	15:46	16:46	17:46	18:46	19:46
Halwill Junction - arrival	10	08:56	09:56	10:56	11:56	12:56	13:56	14:56	15:56	16:56	17:56	18:56	19:56
wait - before departure at	4	09:00	10:00	11:00	12:00	13:00	14:00	15:00	16:00	17:00	18:00	19:00	parked
	60												

Halwill Junction to Launceston: a recreation from the historic timetable

Halwill Junction to Launceston.

Launceston originally had two stations: a Great Western Railway (GWR) one and a London & South West Railway (LSWR) one. They were situated in close proximity to each other on the present site of an industrial estate to the east of the town, the GWR terminus being the northernmost one. The GWR line ended at Launceston. The LSWR continued under a road bridge and on to Wadebridge.

The restoration proposals see the two railway lines approaching Launceston from the east joining into a short single-track line for the last short run into a new Launceston railway platform - *see map.*

The present day industrial estate is well-developed and busy; it would therefore seem unlikely that the occupying businesses would welcome the intrusion of a *through* railway line (as was the LSWR one). Such would require tram-like train movements over the principal road used by the industrial estate and likely would hinder access to their businesses to the extent that it would be resisted or, if built, be detrimental to their continuation and occupation of the industrial units.

Therefore, it would seem logical to explore the potential for an alternative, one which used the more northerly, GWR line as far as the historic GWR station and - this is the key change - a new stretch of railway line onwards to the west and across the north-south road (on a new level crossing); thence along the east-west Riverside Road, crossing the present day bowling club green and thence joining the historic LSWR route - *see map* - on its way to Wadebridge (and Padstow).

As it passed initially through the industrial estate, the line would lie immediately south (and nearly adjoining) the River Kensey (much as the original GWR one did) and would require very little appropriation of existing structures, almost all of which could remain. The location also offers good scope for a station car park.

Note that these proposals would be much better illustrated if superimposed on satellite images rather than the maps of a century ago which illustrate the historic lines. However, the author has no budget to pay for the licensing cost to achieve that. It is hoped that a future edition can include such aerial images.

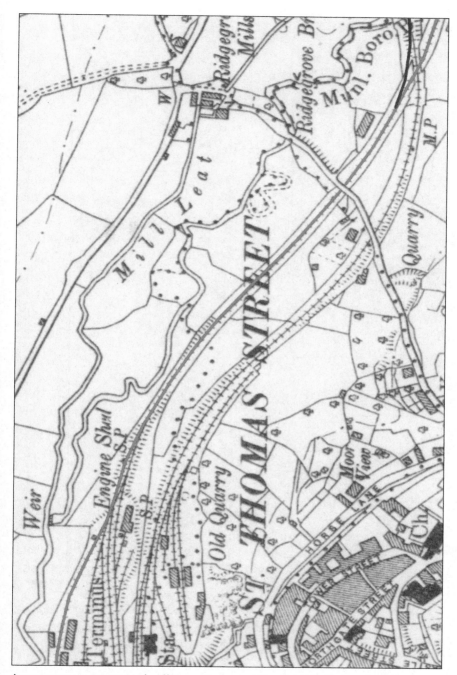

Launceston east, Halwill Junction and Tavistock *lines converge*

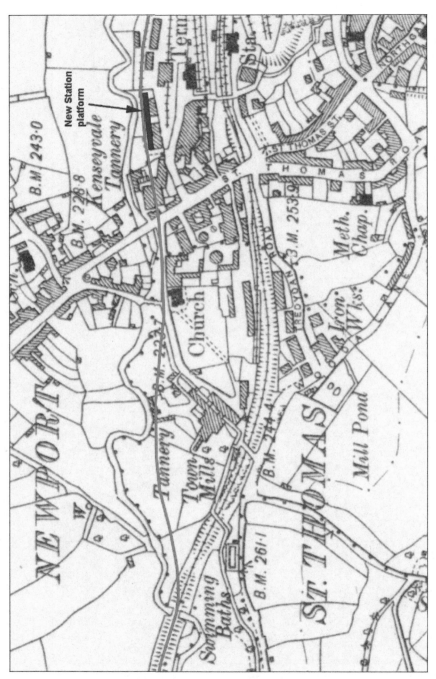

Launceston west, diversion from the historic Wadebridge line

The CORNISH WANDERER (southbound)

11

Launceston - departure	minutes en route	35	miles one way 2 trains 28 mph								01:15 interval	
			08:00	09:15	10:30	11:45	13:00	14:15	15:30	16:45	18:00	19:15
Egloskerry	10		08:10	09:25	10:40	11:55	13:10	14:25	15:40	16:55	18:10	19:25
Tresmeer	8		08:18	09:33	10:48	12:03	13:18	14:33	15:48	17:03	18:18	19:33
Otterham Stn.	10		08:28	09:43	10:58	12:13	13:28	14:43	15:58	17:13	18:28	19:43
The en-route passing place	3		08:31	09:46	11:01	12:16	13:31	14:46	16:01	17:16	18:31	19:46
wait for the other train before departing	2		08:33	09:48	11:03	12:18	13:33	14:48	16:03	17:18	18:33	19:48
Camelford	10		08:43	09:58	11:13	12:28	13:43	14:58	16:13	17:28	18:43	19:58
Delabole	7		08:50	10:05	11:20	12:35	13:50	15:05	16:20	17:35	18:50	20:05
Port Isaac Road	8		08:58	10:13	11:28	12:43	13:58	15:13	16:28	17:43	18:58	20:13
Kew Highway	5		09:03	10:18	11:33	12:48	14:03	15:18	16:33	17:48	19:03	20:18
Wadebridge - arrival	9		09:12	10:27	11:42	12:57	14:12	15:27	16:42	17:57	19:12	20:27
wait - before departure at	3		09:15	10:30	11:45	13:00	14:15	15:30	16:45	18:00	19:15	parked
	75											

The CORNISH WANDERER (northbound)

11

Wadebridge	minutes en route	35	miles one way 2 trains 28 mph								01:15 interval	
			08:00	09:15	10:30	11:45	13:00	14:15	15:30	16:45	18:00	19:15
Kew Highway	9		08:09	09:24	10:39	11:54	13:09	14:24	15:39	16:54	18:09	19:24
Port Isaac Road	5		08:14	09:29	10:44	11:59	13:14	14:29	15:44	16:59	18:14	19:29
Delabole	8		08:22	09:37	10:52	12:07	13:22	14:37	15:52	17:07	18:22	19:37
Camelford	7		08:29	09:44	10:59	12:14	13:29	14:44	15:59	17:14	18:29	19:44
The en-route passing place	3		08:32	09:47	11:02	12:17	13:32	14:47	16:02	17:17	18:32	19:47
wait for the other train before departing	2		08:34	09:49	11:04	12:19	13:34	14:49	16:04	17:19	18:34	19:49
Otterham Stn.	10		08:44	09:59	11:14	12:29	13:44	14:59	16:14	17:29	18:44	19:59
Tresmeer	10		08:54	10:09	11:24	12:39	13:54	15:09	16:24	17:39	18:54	20:09
Egloskerry	8		09:02	10:17	11:32	12:47	14:02	15:17	16:32	17:47	19:02	20:17
Launceston - arrival	10		09:12	10:27	11:42	12:57	14:12	15:27	16:42	17:57	19:12	20:27
wait - before departure at	3		09:15	10:30	11:45	13:00	14:15	15:30	16:45	18:00	19:15	parked
	75											

Launceston to Wadebridge: a recreation from the historic timetable

Wadebridge represents a considerable challenge for railway line restoration, so much so that it raises the fundamental question: *can it really be done?*

The author professes no authoritative answer; indeed, the only one that seems to have merit is that *the railway was there before*. The town is perpetually very busy and, so it seems, every conceivable spare square inch of space is dedicated to car parking.

The original route transited through the town on an east-west axis. In fact, when the train ceased, its trackbed was seized as a road. The station is well preserved and would once again serve perfectly well.

The topology of the area and the River Camel within it all made the original LSWR designer's task tricky; the subsequent development makes restoration even more so; indeed, an alternative to the east-west transit cannot be identified by the author.

Amsterdam tram: it's worth showing this photo again; if Amsterdam can live with trams sharing the road with vehicles then surely Wadebridge can do so as well.

Restoration of an east-west thru-train would be, essentially, an exercise in managing road use and limitation with restrictions. From the east, Guineaport Road would become one-way for road traffic to the restored Station and then as far as Southern Way, which would also become one-way for traffic; along Jubilee Road and Eddystone Road the railway line would occupy one half of the width of these roads too, rendering them both one-way streets. Ultimately, the railway would emerge from the town to resume its route on the Camel Trail to Padstow.

A number of level crossings would be required where roads bisect Guineaport Rd, Jubilee Rd, Southern Way and Eddystone Rd. These would be controlled by traffic lights.

This is a possibility worth exploring but it is not a detailed design; such is far beyond the limited or outline scope of this paper.

Whether the people of Wadebridge and the Council representing them would wish to see such a substantive change, despite the gains in affordable housing that would result (and mainline rail connectivity), would be the ultimate question hanging over the prospects for both the Launceston-Wadebridge-Padstow and Bodmin-Wadebridge-Padstow lines; indeed it is the question that will influence the public reception for restored railway lines more generally.

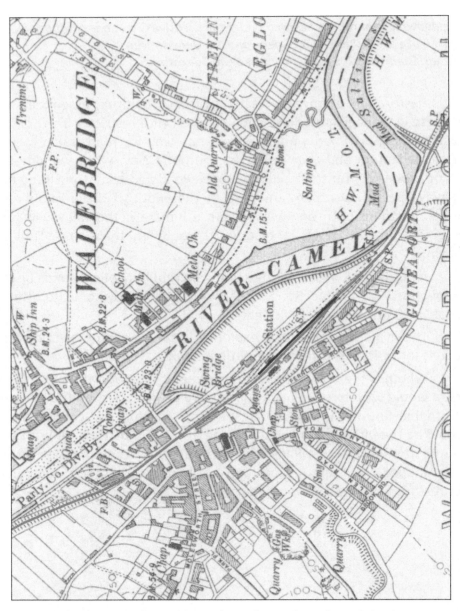

Wadebridge town transit can be achieved on the original route.
The original station is re-opened

Padstow, relative to Wadebridge, is a far easier problem for railway restoration (assuming that Wadebridge could be negotiated); the original track-bed, *now the Camel Trail,* from Wadebridge would be used, but the line would terminate short of the preserved old railway station - *see map.*

The suggested new (and simple) platform would be located on the site of a length of industrial buildings, including the Quay Garage vehicle workshop. The site already offers a very good car park.

Padstow would be the terminus for a restored heritage steam train, the **Atlantic Coast Express**, coming all the way from Taunton (one which would certainly be popular with tourists). The train would take about five and a half hours and offer a premium lunch service aboard before its passengers ultimately alighted in Padstow for one or more nights in its hostelries, bringing many patrons to the dining institutions of the town. It is a journey which could not offer a same-day return; the return to Taunton would be on the following day (or succeeding days); thus, patronage for the town's hotels and restaurants would be assured. Padstow's counterpart, **Rock**, on the opposite side of the River Camel, would also benefit because passengers could cross on the ferry to patronise its hotels.

THE PADSTOW PULLMAN	minutes	16			miles one way		24 mph		1 train	01:30	cycle
	en route										
Padstow			08:00	09:30	11:00	12:30	14:00	15:30	17:00	18:30	20:00
Wadebridge	9		08:09	09:39	11:09	12:39	14:09	15:39	17:09	18:39	20:09
Grogley Halt	7		08:16	09:46	11:16	12:46	14:16	15:46	17:16	18:46	20:16
Nanstallon Halt	4		08:20	09:50	11:20	12:50	14:20	15:50	17:20	18:50	20:20
Bodmin General - arrival	9		08:29	09:59	11:29	12:59	14:29	15:59	17:29	18:59	20:29
wait - before departure at	3		08:32	10:02	11:32	13:02	14:32	16:02	17:32	19:02	20:32
Bodmin Parkway (Road) - arrival	7		08:39	10:09	11:39	13:09	14:39	16:09	17:39	19:09	20:39
wait - before departure at	4		08:43	10:13	11:43	13:13	14:43	16:13	17:43	19:13	20:43
Bodmin General - arrival	7		08:50	10:20	11:50	13:20	14:50	16:20	17:50	19:20	20:50
wait - before departure at	3		08:53	10:23	11:53	13:23	14:53	16:23	17:53	19:23	20:53
Nanstallon Halt	9		09:02	10:32	12:02	13:32	15:02	16:32	18:02	19:32	21:02
Grogley Halt	4		09:06	10:36	12:06	13:36	15:06	16:36	18:06	19:36	21:06
Wadebridge	7		09:13	10:43	12:13	13:43	15:13	16:43	18:13	19:43	21:13
Padstow - arrival	9		09:22	10:52	12:22	13:52	15:22	16:52	18:22	19:52	21:22
wait - before departure at	8		09:30	11:00	12:30	14:00	15:30	17:00	18:30	20:00	parked
	90										

Padstow to Bodmin Parkway (main line) via
Wadebridge: a recreation from the historic timetable

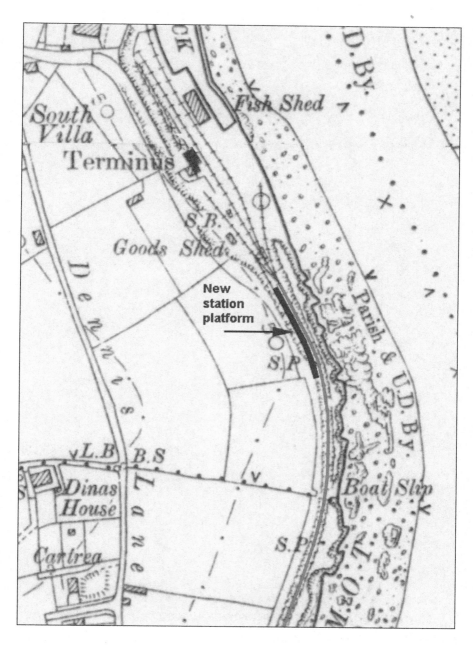

New Padstow station platform

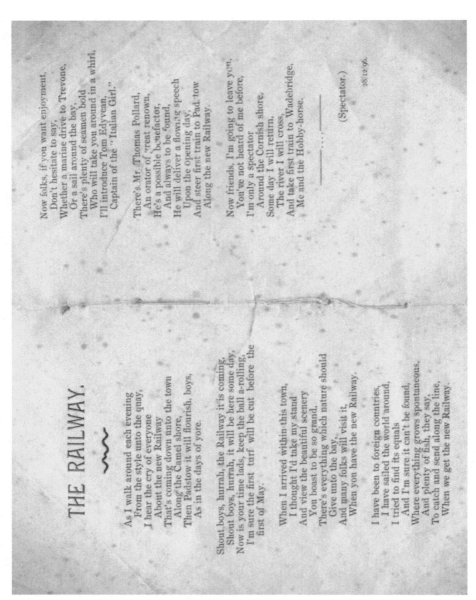

THE RAILWAY.

As I walk around each evening
From the style unto the quay,
I hear the cry of everyone
About the new Railway
That's coming down unto the town
Along the Camel shore,
Then Padstow it will flourish, boys,
As in the days of yore.

Shout boys, hurrah, the Railway it is coming,
Shout boys, hurrah, it will be here some day,
Now is your time lads, keep the ball a-rolling,
I'm sure the first turf will be cut before the
first of May.

When I arrived within this town,
I thought I'd take my stand
And view the beautiful scenery
You boast to be so grand.
There's everything which nature should
Give unto the bay,
And many folks will visit it,
When you have the new Railway.

I have been to foreign countries,
I have sailed the world around,
I tried to find its equals
And I'm sure it can't be found,
Where everything grows spontaneous,
And plenty of fish, they say,
To catch and send along the line,
When we get the new Railway.

Now folks, if you want enjoyment,
Don't hesitate to say,
Whether a marine drive to Trevone,
Or a sail around the bay,
There's plenty of seamen bold
Who will take you around in a whirl,
I'll introduce Tom Edyvean,
Captain of the "Italian Girl."

There's Mr. Thomas Pollard,
An orator of great renown,
He's a possible benefactor,
And always to be found,
He will deliver a flowing speech
Upon the opening day,
And steer first train to Padstow
Along the new Railway.

Now friends, I'm going to leave you,
You've not heard of me before,
I'm only a spectator
Around the Cornish shore,
Some day I will return,
The river I will cross,
And take first train to Wadebridge,
Me and the Hobby-horse.

(Spectator.)

28/12/96.

source: http://www.northcornwallrailway.co.uk/

Might the population of Padstow once again look forward to another poem to inaugurate a restored railway?

Returning to **Halwill Junction**, the Exeter connection for the three lines entering the station from the north would be the Okehampton line. A (relatively) frequent service of one train per hour would be available. The journey would take 30 minutes.

From Okehampton, passengers could take the existing, recently restored in November 2021, line to Exeter * or a *restored* line to a *restored* Tavistock (*North*) platform for onward journey to Bere Regis and Plymouth.

* The restoration has been a great success: the number of passenger journeys has been double what was expected in the months since opening up to August 2022, and 120,000 journeys have been made. **

** source: *https://www.bbc.co.uk/news/uk-england-devon-62736152*

In fact they could also disembark the Tavistock line at Lydford Junction and then board a train also bearing south but to a new platform for Tavistock (*South*), from where the line continues to a *restored* Yelverton Junction, where they could switch to a train for a *restored* Princetown platform or simply continue to Marsh Mills, and ultimately terminate at Plymouth (North Road, as it was named before).

The long and meandering restored line from Plymouth via Marsh Mills to Yelverton Junction, to Okehampton, to Halwill Junction, Torrington, Bideford, Barnstaple and on to terminate at Ilfracombe would be the route for another *heritage steam* train, the "**Devon Belle**", offering steam enthusiasts a marvellous journey through the glorious scenery of Devon from south to north; and also offering a stimulus to the hotels of Ilfracombe who, potentially, might see that as a better alternative to asylum-seekers.

A short steam train journey from Yelverton Junction to a restored Princetown platform would undoubtedly appeal to steam enthusiasts. The DMU service for the same route would much facilitate commuting from Princetown to Plymouth and vice versa.

13

The JUNCTION EXPRESS

The JUNCTION EXPRESS	minutes en route		miles one way				1 train		01:00	cycle		22 mph	
Okehampton - departure		08:00	09:00	10:00	11:00	12:00	13:00	14:00	15:00	16:00	17:00	18:00	19:00
Maddaford Moor	12	08:12	09:12	10:12	11:12	12:12	13:12	14:12	15:12	16:12	17:12	18:12	19:12
Ashbury	8	08:20	09:20	10:20	11:20	12:20	13:20	14:20	15:20	16:20	17:20	18:20	19:20
Halwill Junction - arrival	8	08:28	09:28	10:28	11:28	12:28	13:28	14:28	15:28	16:28	17:28	18:28	19:28
wait - before departure at	2	08:30	09:30	10:30	11:30	12:30	13:30	14:30	15:30	16:30	17:30	18:30	19:30
Ashbury	8	08:38	09:38	10:38	11:38	12:38	13:38	14:38	15:38	16:38	17:38	18:38	19:38
Maddaford Moor	8	08:46	09:46	10:46	11:46	12:46	13:46	14:46	15:46	16:46	17:46	18:46	19:46
Okehampton - arrival	12	08:58	09:58	10:58	11:58	12:58	13:58	14:58	15:58	16:58	17:58	18:58	19:58
wait - before departure at	2	09:00	10:00	11:00	12:00	13:00	14:00	15:00	16:00	17:00	18:00	19:00	parked
	60												

Okehampton to Halwill Junction: a recreation from the historic timetable

14

The WESTERLY FRINGE

	minutes en route	24		miles one way	1 train	25 mph	02:00	cycle
Okehampton - departure		08:00	10:00	12:00	14:00	16:00	18:00	20:00
Bridestowe	15	08:15	10:15	12:15	14:15	16:15	18:15	20:15
Lydford Jcn.	7	08:22	10:22	12:22	14:22	16:22	18:22	20:22
wait - before departure at	3	08:25	10:25	12:25	14:25	16:25	18:25	20:25
Brentor	5	08:30	10:30	12:30	14:30	16:30	18:30	20:30
Mary Tavy & Blackdown	3	08:33	10:33	12:33	14:33	16:33	18:33	20:33
Tavistock North	8	08:41	10:41	12:41	14:41	16:41	18:41	20:41
Bere Alston - arrival	14	08:55	10:55	12:55	14:55	16:55	18:55	20:55
wait - before departure at	5	09:00	11:00	13:00	15:00	17:00	19:00	21:00
Tavistock North	14	09:14	11:14	13:14	15:14	17:14	19:14	21:14
Mary Tavy & Blackdown	8	09:22	11:22	13:22	15:22	17:22	19:22	21:22
Brentor	3	09:25	11:25	13:25	15:25	17:25	19:25	21:25
Lydford Jcn.	5	09:30	11:30	13:30	15:30	17:30	19:30	21:30
wait - before departure at	3	09:33	11:33	13:33	15:33	17:33	19:33	21:33
Bridestowe	7	09:40	11:40	13:40	15:40	17:40	19:40	21:40
Okehampton - arrival	15	09:55	11:55	13:55	15:55	17:55	19:55	21:55
wait - before departure at	5	10:00	12:00	14:00	16:00	18:00	20:00	parked
	120							

Okehampton to Tavistock (North) and Bere Alston: a recreation from the historic timetable

Tavistock, historically, enjoyed two railway lines, and each had a station to serve them. Current day plans moot restoration of a railway to the south; however, restoration to Okehampton would, unfortunately, appear to have been written off; this seems *to the author* to be another repetition of shortsightedness.

The LSWR line from Okehampton (to Devonport and Plymouth) was served by Tavistock (North) and the GWR line from Launceston (also to Plymouth, via Marsh Mills) was served by Tavistock (South).

The historic LSWR line is the subject of the *present day* push for restoration; from the town (centre?) it continues south-west to Bere Alston, from where today's operational branch line would enable a Plymouth connection. *Has a Tavistock North station been written off?*

The GWR line (the former Tavistock South station) is presently wholly absent of such restoration interest; however, the potentially significant benefits of restoration are several:

1. the indicated location of a new Tavistock (South) platform is more favourable for car parking than a restored Tavistock (North) station,
2. it would (via Yelverton) enable Princetown, on Dartmoor, to be once again connected to the railway (undoubtedly that would be popular with tourists), and
3. it would also offer a rail service to residents of Horrabridge and Yelverton.

A restored Tavistock (North station) line would shave the perimeter of the Mid-Devon District Council building as it passed by from the north in a loop to gain the preserved old station (the platform of which would be returned to service). Unfortunately a small housing development (Quant Park) straddles the old track-bed just before it reaches the bridge over Drake Road; unfortunately, that would necessitate demolition of those 10 houses.

Generally-stated, there are more obstacles to restoration on the Tavistock (South station) railway, including clinics, the fire and police stations and apartment blocks, as well as one significant industrial unit further south which sits astride the historic line (and which would require demolition). However, the restored line route could conceivably be 'squeezed in', a little east of its original route, to (just about) bypass the clinics, fire and police stations and the apartments. Obviously, more detailed study would be required; this is a simplistic statement.

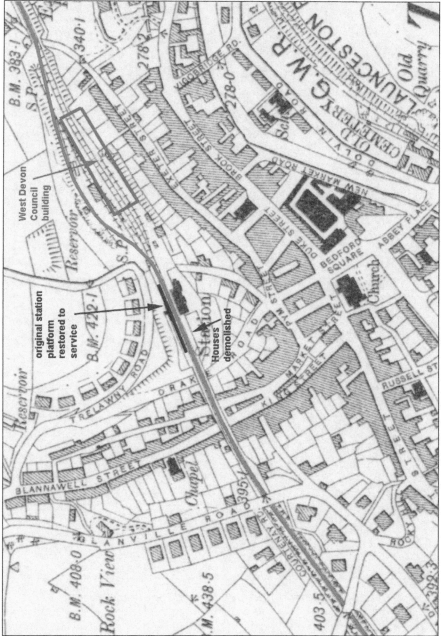

Tavistock (North) house demolitions, new station (platform)

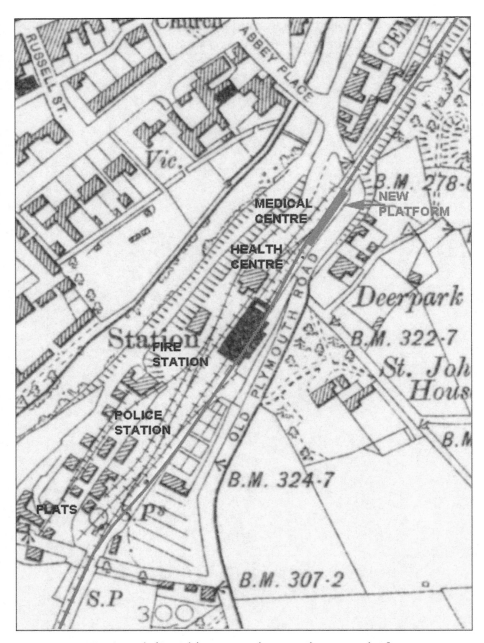

Tavistock (South) approaches, and a new platform

STAGE ONE 15

The TAVY TRANSIT - route cycle

	minutes			miles one way	1 train	25 mph		01:45	cycle
	en route	08:00	09:45	11:30	13:15	15:00	16:45	18:30	20:15
Launceston - departure	10	08:00	09:45	11:30	13:15	15:00	16:45	18:30	20:15
Lifton	8	08:10	09:55	11:40	13:25	15:10	16:55	18:40	20:25
Coryton	13	08:18	10:03	11:48	13:33	15:18	17:03	18:48	20:33
Lydford Junction - arrival	2	08:31	10:16	12:01	13:46	15:31	17:16	19:01	20:46
wait - before departure at		08:33	10:18	12:03	13:48	15:33	17:18	19:03	20:48
Brentor	5	08:38	10:23	12:08	13:53	15:38	17:23	19:08	20:53
Mary Tavy & Blackdown	3	08:41	10:26	12:11	13:56	15:41	17:26	19:11	20:56
Tavistock South	8	08:49	10:34	12:19	14:04	15:49	17:34	19:19	21:04
wait - before departure at	3	08:52	10:37	12:22	14:07	15:52	17:37	19:22	21:07
Mary Tavy & Blackdown	8	09:00	10:45	12:30	14:15	16:00	17:45	19:30	21:15
Brentor	3	09:03	10:48	12:33	14:18	16:03	17:48	19:33	21:18
Lydford Junction - arrival	5	09:08	10:53	12:38	14:23	16:08	17:53	19:38	21:23
wait - before departure at	2	09:10	10:55	12:40	14:25	16:10	17:55	19:40	21:25
Coryton	13	09:23	11:08	12:53	14:38	16:23	18:08	19:53	21:38
Lifton	8	09:31	11:16	13:01	14:46	16:31	18:16	20:01	21:46
Launceston - arrival	10	09:41	11:26	13:11	14:56	16:41	18:26	20:11	21:56
wait - before departure at	4	09:45	11:30	13:15	15:00	16:45	18:30	20:15	*parked*
	105								

Launceston to Tavistock (South): a recreation from the historic timetable

STAGE ONE 16

The JANNER - route cycle	minutes en route	08:00	09:40	11:20 miles one way	13:00 1 train	14:40 23 mph	16:20	01:40 18:00	cycle 19:40
Tavistock South - departure		08:00	09:40	11:20	13:00	14:40	16:20	18:00	19:40
Whitchurch Down	3	08:03	09:43	11:23	13:03	14:43	16:23	18:03	19:43
Horrobridge	7	08:10	09:50	11:30	13:10	14:50	16:30	18:10	19:50
Yelverton Junction - arrival	5	08:15	09:55	11:35	13:15	14:55	16:35	18:15	19:55
wait - before departure at	3	08:18	09:58	11:38	13:18	14:58	16:38	18:18	19:58
Clearbrook Halt	3	08:21	10:01	11:41	13:21	15:01	16:41	18:21	20:01
Shaugh Bridge	3	08:24	10:04	11:44	13:24	15:04	16:44	18:24	20:04
Bickleigh	5	08:29	10:09	11:49	13:29	15:09	16:49	18:29	20:09
Plym Bridge	5	08:34	10:14	11:54	13:34	15:14	16:54	18:34	20:14
Marsh Mills	4	08:38	10:18	11:58	13:38	15:18	16:58	18:38	20:18
Plymouth (North Road) - arrival	8	08:46	10:26	12:06	13:46	15:26	17:06	18:46	20:26
wait - before departure at	4	08:50	10:30	12:10	13:50	15:30	17:10	18:50	20:30
Marsh Mills	8	08:58	10:38	12:18	13:58	15:38	17:18	18:58	20:38
Plym Bridge	4	09:02	10:42	12:22	14:02	15:42	17:22	19:02	20:42
Bickleigh	5	09:07	10:47	12:27	14:07	15:47	17:27	19:07	20:47
Shaugh Bridge	5	09:12	10:52	12:32	14:12	15:52	17:32	19:12	20:52
Clearbrook Halt	3	09:15	10:55	12:35	14:15	15:55	17:35	19:15	20:55
Yelverton Junction - arrival	3	09:18	10:58	12:38	14:18	15:58	17:38	19:18	20:58
wait - before departure at	3	09:21	11:01	12:41	14:21	16:01	17:41	19:21	21:01
Horrobridge	5	09:26	11:06	12:46	14:26	16:06	17:46	19:26	21:06
Whitchurch Down	7	09:33	11:13	12:53	14:33	16:13	17:53	19:33	21:13
Tavistock South	3	09:36	11:16	12:56	14:36	16:16	17:56	19:36	21:16
wait - before departure at	4	09:40	11:20	13:00	14:40	16:20	18:00	19:40	parked
	100								

Tavistock (South) to Marsh Mills (main line) via Yelverton Junction, a restored Tavistock Junction and thence to Plymouth: a recreation from the historic timetable

The TAVY TRANSIT / JANNER (southbound)

38.5 miles one way · 2 trains 23 mph · 01:40 interval

	minutes en route	08:00	09:40	11:20	13:00	14:40	16:20	18:00	19:40 interval
Launceston - departure		08:00	09:40	11:20	13:00	14:40	16:20	18:00	19:40
Lifton	10	08:10	09:50	11:30	13:10	14:50	16:30	18:10	19:50
Coryton	8	08:18	09:58	11:38	13:18	14:58	16:38	18:18	19:58
Lydford Junction - arrival	13	08:31	10:11	11:51	13:31	15:11	16:51	18:31	20:11
wait - before departure at	2	08:33	10:13	11:53	13:33	15:13	16:53	18:33	20:13
Brentor	5	08:38	10:18	11:58	13:38	15:18	16:58	18:38	20:18
Mary Tavy & Blackdown	3	08:41	10:21	12:01	13:41	15:21	17:01	18:41	20:21
Tavistock South	8	08:49	10:29	12:09	13:49	15:29	17:09	18:49	20:29
wait - before departure at	2	08:51	10:31	12:11	13:51	15:31	17:11	18:51	20:31
Whitchurch Down	3	08:54	10:34	12:14	13:54	15:34	17:14	18:54	20:34
Horrobridge	7	09:01	10:41	12:21	14:01	15:41	17:21	19:01	20:41
Yelverton Junction - arrival	5	09:06	10:46	12:26	14:06	15:46	17:26	19:06	20:46
wait - before departure at	3	09:09	10:49	12:29	14:09	15:49	17:29	19:09	20:49
Clearbrook Halt	3	09:12	10:52	12:32	14:12	15:52	17:32	19:12	20:52
Shaugh Bridge	3	09:15	10:55	12:35	14:15	15:55	17:35	19:15	20:55
Bickleigh	5	09:20	11:00	12:40	14:20	16:00	17:40	19:20	21:00
Plym Bridge	5	09:25	11:05	12:45	14:25	16:05	17:45	19:25	21:05
Marsh Mills	4	09:29	11:09	12:49	14:29	16:09	17:49	19:29	21:09
Plymouth (North Road) - arrival	8	09:37	11:17	12:57	14:37	16:17	17:57	19:37	21:17
wait - before departure at	3	09:40	11:20	13:00	14:40	16:20	18:00	19:40	parked
	100								

Launceston to Plymouth via Marsh Mills, via Yelverton Junction and Tavistock (South): a recreation from the historic timetable

STAGE TWO 15 (and 16) combined

The TAVY TRANSIT / JANNER (northbound)	minutes en route	38.5	miles one way 2 trains 23 mph					01:40	interval
Plymouth (North Road) - departure		08:00	09:40	11:20	13:00	14:40	16:20	18:00	19:40
Marsh Mills	8	08:08	09:48	11:28	13:08	14:48	16:28	18:08	19:48
Plym Bridge	4	08:12	09:52	11:32	13:12	14:52	16:32	18:12	19:52
Bickleigh	5	08:17	09:57	11:37	13:17	14:57	16:37	18:17	19:57
Shaugh Bridge	5	08:22	10:02	11:42	13:22	15:02	16:42	18:22	20:02
Clearbrook Halt	3	08:25	10:05	11:45	13:25	15:05	16:45	18:25	20:05
Yelverton Junction - arrival	3	08:28	10:08	11:48	13:28	15:08	16:48	18:28	20:08
wait - before departure at	3	08:31	10:11	11:51	13:31	15:11	16:51	18:31	20:11
Horrobridge	5	08:36	10:16	11:56	13:36	15:16	16:56	18:36	20:16
Whitchurch Down	7	08:43	10:23	12:03	13:43	15:23	17:03	18:43	20:23
Tavistock South	3	08:46	10:26	12:06	13:46	15:26	17:06	18:46	20:26
wait - before departure at	2	08:48	08:48	08:48	08:48	08:48	08:48	08:48	08:48
Mary Tavy & Blackdown	8	08:56	10:36	12:16	13:56	15:36	17:16	18:56	20:36
Brentor	3	08:59	10:39	12:19	13:59	15:39	17:19	18:59	20:39
Lydford Junction - arrival	5	09:04	10:44	12:24	14:04	15:44	17:24	19:04	20:44
wait - before departure at	2	09:06	10:46	12:26	14:06	15:46	17:26	19:06	20:46
Coryton	13	09:19	10:59	12:39	14:19	15:59	17:39	19:19	20:59
Lifton	8	09:27	11:07	12:47	14:27	16:07	17:47	19:27	21:07
Launceston - arrival	10	09:37	11:17	12:57	14:37	16:17	17:57	19:37	21:17
wait - before departure at	3	09:40	11:20	13:00	14:40	16:20	18:00	19:40	parked
	100								

Plymouth to Launceston via Marsh Mills via Yelverton Junction and Tavistock (South): a recreation from the historic timetable

17

The DARTMOOR ROVER

	minutes	10.5	miles one way	1 train	20 mph			01:30	cycle
Princetown - departure	en route	08:00	09:30	11:00	12:30	14:00	15:30	17:00	18:30
King Tor Halt	5	08:05	09:35	11:05	12:35	14:05	15:35	17:05	18:35
Ingra Tor Halt	9	08:14	09:44	11:14	12:44	14:14	15:44	17:14	18:44
Burrator Halt	11	08:25	09:55	11:25	12:55	14:25	15:55	17:25	18:55
Dousland	5	08:30	10:00	11:30	13:00	14:30	16:00	17:30	19:00
Yelverton Jcn. - arrival	5	08:35	10:05	11:35	13:05	14:35	16:05	17:35	19:05
wait - before departure at	10	08:45	10:15	11:45	13:15	14:45	16:15	17:45	19:15
Dousland	5	08:50	10:20	11:50	13:20	14:50	16:20	17:50	19:20
Burrator Halt	5	08:55	10:25	11:55	13:25	14:55	16:25	17:55	19:25
Ingra Tor Halt	11	09:06	10:36	12:06	13:36	15:06	16:36	18:06	19:36
King Tor Halt	9	09:15	10:45	12:15	13:45	15:15	16:45	18:15	19:45
Princetown - arrival	5	09:20	10:50	12:20	13:50	15:20	16:50	18:20	19:50
wait - before departure at	10	09:30	11:00	12:30	14:00	15:30	17:00	18:30	parked
	90								

Princetown to Yelverton Junction: a recreation from the historic timetable

Devon for sunshine!

MONTHLY RETURN TICKETS
· PENNY · A · MILE ·
ISSUED ALL THE YEAR ROUND

GWR 1935 poster   A penny a mile!

Tariffs and passenger payment

A penny a mile! Tickets on restored railway lines are unlikely to be so cheap *(perhaps)*, but the cost of travel for the Cornish man could well be less than the use of a car.

A penny (1d / 240 of them to the pound) in 1936 would be equivalent to about 31p today (2022). Hence 31p per mile for the Devon journey from (say) Barnstaple to Ilfracombe (15 miles) would cost (in today's figures) £4.65; which does not sound extravagant (*but only as a one-off*). A week's train commuting would cost £46.50, and a full year of such commuting (45 weeks) equates to £2,092. This looks expensive for the commuter and, given the stated appeal of the train to the less well-off, it's hardly convincing.

This compares with 150 miles per week of motoring, the fuel cost of which would be: 30mpg/4.5 litres (each day) x 5 days x £1.80/litre = £40.50.

Of course the true cost of the car is more: the 'fixed' costs of car tax, insurance, MOT test, maintenance and the amortisation of the car cost might realistically total in excess of £2,200 per year*, or £42 per week / £6 per day; making the comparison much more favourable for the train; indeed, the train begins to look like a bargain - but only for a one-person commuter trip or, at most, two persons; but the numbers tilt towards the car as soon as a third person is involved.

* car tax £150, insurance £350, MOT £25, maintenance (tyres etc) £250, amortisation £1,500 (at least, unless an 'old banger') = £2,200

Another comparison: Taunton to Barnstaple (49 miles) would be £15.19 per person at a train fare of 31p per mile; so, a short-break return journey from Taunton, a leisurely transit across Exmoor and its scenery, to Barnstaple would cost £30.38. *NB this is for one person.* The train time would be almost 2 hours (militating against the commuter but suggesting it would primarily be a journey for tourists).

The car alternative would be faster (just over one hour) but less appealing: 98 miles. The fuel consumed and its cost would be (at 42 mpg) 2.33 gallons or 10.6 litres and (at £1.85 per litre) £19.64 - just two-thirds of the train fare. Furthermore, the car could transport the family, and so the car is actually significantly cheaper than the train when it was priced at "one (old, 1936) penny per mile". This is the inherent contrast, the problem for the train is always going to be the cost relative to the car *with more than one person in it*, and the choice to be made by the traveller will often depend on cost as well as time.

The comparison is therefore far less favourable for the train when children are travelling too: the car absorbs their travel cost. Perhaps therein lies a clue for the future railway marketing department: the parents pay and the kids (under 18) travel free?

For couples taking a 'leisure break', a return train fare of (in the order of) £25 per person (20p per mile) might well prove suitably attractive. **Can this be achieved?**

Does such a fare as 20p per mile also suit the commuter?

A **Barnstaple - Ilfracombe** weekly commute (return journey, 5 days) would equate to 15 miles each way x 5 days = 150 miles travelled, which equates to a weekly return ticket of £30. The fuel for a car (16.23 litres) would also cost precisely £30. As the car commuter would have the usual fixed overhead car costs and probably also have to pay for parking, the railway commute would make sense.

How much to charge passengers?

In the summer of 2022 the German government introduced a promotional rail pass which offered unlimited national rail travel for just nine euros.

source: The Guardian 3rd Nov.

https://www.theguardian.com/world/2022/nov/03/row-over-germanys-public-transport-ticket-jumping-from-9-to-49

There is a vigorous debate about what should succeed it; forty-nine euros has been proposed, beginning in January 2023; Berlin has also suggested a twenty-nine euros pass within only its own region. The subsidy, nationally, for a forty-nine euros monthly rail ticket is estimated at three billion euros (which seems extremely unlikely to fly in either Whitehall, Devon or Cornwall).

Should rail or indeed any public transport be subsidised?

Rural buses have been for a long time. The principle of subsidy is understood and accepted. Should it apply to rail travel? And who is to pay for subsidies? The answers are beyond the author's ken.

It is worth noting that in Luxembourg (admittedly the smallest of the EU states) all public transport is free. **Is this a Utopian ideal?**

For the summer months of June, July and August 2022 the German government introduced a nine euros monthly transport pass; the result was a broad increase of about 50% in train travel and a decline in car use in 23 of 26 German cities. *

* source:
https://www.theguardian.com/world/2022/jul/14/germany-9-euro-travel-pass-cheap-fares

It must be remembered that such offers appeal to persons who have ready access to a train service, but for everyone who does not (such as the majority of people in the rural areas, villages and small towns of northern Devon and Cornwall) then the appeal is limited; it is still necessary to reach (by car and to park) at the most convenient railway station; and that, in north Devon, is either Barnstaple or (for journeys further afield) Tiverton Parkway. For this reason, restoration of a wider regional rural railway network is essential if car use is ever to significantly diminish and, in these straightened times for the less affluent of society, travel itself is to remain feasible at all. In short, only a far more extensive network of rural lines which are (*important this*) operated on behalf of communities by communities and which remain affordable to use and to operate will provide the mechanism to boost community cohesiveness and connectivity to and from the rest of the UK (*which is so very valuable for tourism*).

In September 2022 the Spanish government offered a 50% discount on 41 intercity bus routes and, from 1st February 2023 free travel on Madrid - Barcelona buses, expected to be extended to all long and medium distance routes. In respect of rail travel a similar scheme was introduced concurrently but with free travel since September 2022 except for the high-speed lines where passengers could qualify for a 50% discount, all schemes running until the end of 2023. *

source: https://www.theguardian.com/world/2023/jan/05/spain-expands-free-travel-offer-to-intercity-bus-services

It can be seen, therefore, that at least some European governments are profoundly re-evaluating the contribution of public transport, rail particularly, to their economies, to the extent that subsidy is considered equally beneficial if applied to rail travel as it is to road transportation.

It is perhaps unfortunate that in 2022 the price of UK rail tickets was increased. Is this counter-productive? In some UK rural areas some single-way bus tickets cost as much as £5. This seems unlikely to persuade anyone with a choice to forego the car.

The oft-ignored but beneficial aspect of rail travel is the reduction of pollution, of CO_2 and noxious gases. In the short term, a reintroduced rail service in rural Davon and Cornwall would necessarily rely on the diesel engines of multiple-units (DMUs); however, ultimately, the prospect for electrification will be at hand: non-polluting, overhead catenary wiring.

How could such an low-cost rail operation, offering discounts or even free travel, conceivably be sustainable here in the (relatively poor and low population density) south-west region? Initially, that seems most unlikely.

However, a **DaCSTaR** monthly rail pass of, for example, £10 - were the network to be restored - would undoubtedly be popular. An alternative might be a £1 - go anywhere - ticket: a swift tap of a card and a sum which is affordable for just about everyone is paid. But what are the operating economics likely to be? This preliminary paper cannot possibly answer such questions, but it offers the seeds for further consideration, to the extent of providing possibly viable methodologies.

How to physically charge train passengers?

The question of how and when to charge for train fares is not one that the author has, todate, greatly considered. Various options obviously exist, including: a station ticket office (not the best option given infrequent trains and low volume of passengers at some halts - an alternative would seem desirable), the train conductor or guard (but how to handle a voluminous passenger boarding of multiple carriages at a larger station might be open to fallibility), an unmonitored card swipe (which would assume a unitary fare and depend on honesty), or even a free service (at least on the timetabled DMU trains; certainly debatable, subjective, for where does the funding come from? Perhaps an unlikely choice too.)

For the relatively *small* trains likely to be suited to the routes within this paper, one approach might be to consider the single-carriage DMU as *akin to a bus*: passengers would board and alight only at a single door where the driver would supervise every passenger tapping a card on a payment machine.

With a degree of imagination it is possible to consider electrified trains operating automatically *without any driver at all*. It is perfectly feasible on the simplest end to end lines - out and back, no points, no signals, no passing etc. and few or even no safety hazards when all level-crossings are similarly automatic. It exists: the Gatwick monorail between the North and South terminals (admittedly a very short railway); but with such prospects there will be great scope to minimise costs, reduce subsidy and provide a more sustainable rail network for the rural areas, villages and small towns of Devon and Cornwall.

Self-driving buses are already here. There is a trial about to start on 15th May 2023 with buses crossing the Firth of Forth road bridge without drivers, travelling a 14-miles route. It's no surprise to record that a standby driver will be in the driver's seat until the success or otherwise of this (I will say) *imaginative* concept is proven. However, in the sense of a relatively rural small train operating on a line without other trains and travelling buffer-to-buffer (end to end of the line) where there are no traffic conflicts (other than automatic level-crossings) it might be thought that the automated train is very much safer than an automated bus on a busy road (with drivers of varying expertise to say the least). In fact, the train ticket collector or guard or 'train captain' could serve as the standby driver of an automatic train.*

Unmanned rural halts would abound throughout the network, mandating ticket sales via the train crew. Photo: Bernard Mills.

The passenger capacity of a single-carriage DMU is 65 persons, which is about the lower limit of a modern double-decker bus (60-80 passengers). Significantly, the DMU would have many less stops than a bus, and so this operation would seem to be well within the capacity of a driver; after all, he has no other traffic to be concerned about; nor, indeed, even a steering wheel; besides which, the bus driver is not taking fares when driving, only when stopped; and presumably therefore so too could a DMU driver. It's some way off for trains generally, no doubt, but there are trains which operate *even without a driver* - at airports for example. The Gatwick North-South terminals monorail is one example.

When the DMU reached its *terminus*, all doors would open, the DMU would be entirely vacated, the train would generally be waiting for several minutes before next departure and before which time boarding would commence once more via the single door near the driver.

For two-carriage DMUs, the driver alone might still suffice; but, if not, a conductor or guard could attend the single boarding door in the second carriage. For three-carriage and four-carriage (probably relatively rare) DMUs, a single guard and still two doors only for boarding and alighting at stations along the route might well also suffice (all doors still opening when the terminus is reached).

Were passengers to be charged on the basis of (for example) a pound (or £1.50 or £2, whatever) on boarding the train, that fare would take them as far as that station where they exited the train; it's a simple system and one that the train driver (and guard) can effectively police, as described above. The challenge of such a basis, a unitary fare, is to create a fair charging structure; to do so means that anyone changing trains (lines), generally for a longer journey, would pay again when they boarded successive trains.

This favours the passenger for longer single-train journeys compared with shorter ones. It may be that for the longer trips such as Barnstaple to Taunton, for example, passengers may be charged again at the halfway station (Dulverton). Whether they might be asked to alight and re-board the train is another question, likely doubtful; however, before any passengers were to be admitted at Dulverton, perhaps the guard might pass through the carriages and charge seated passengers before the train admits anyone else (who pays the driver *etc*) for the onward journey.

In this concept, as in many aspects of the operation of such a network, successful acceptance by passengers will follow informative explanations of why such practices are adopted by the network. £1.50

or £2 for Barnstaple to Dulverton is a bargain; another £1.50 or £2 to proceed to Taunton is also a bargain; passengers could not conceivably object to the tariff; inconvenience - specifically, the lack of it - is the key factor.

At the time of writing (spring 2023) the government has adopted a (£60m cost) policy of subsidising bus passengers nationally (where the bus operator accedes to the programme) with £2 fares. More than 130 bus operators have signed up. This is a short term offering and runs for three months only. It is projected to replace 2 million car journeys. *

In London, single bus fares are only £1.65.

The bus subsidy cheme has been made available in Cornwall with a government subsidy of £23.6 million, and a significant increase in bus passengers has resulted. However, the steep inflationary rises in many day to day costs of living may also be a factor, driving people away from cars with fuel prices so very much higher. If this is the case then the case for improved public transport *on a permanant basis* is much the stronger.

* *source: https://www.theguardian.com/money/2022/dec/19/2-cap-for-many-bus-fares-in-england-expected-to-save-2m-car-journeys*

The economic benefits of restoration: illustrations

At the time of writing (8th November 2022) the local builder's merchant, from whom the author has long purchased a considerable amount of materials, has announced its imminent closure on Friday 11th November. The Travis Perkins depots at Stibb Cross and Bude are closing, leaving only Barnstaple. No alternative employment has been made available to the redundant employees.

It is tantalising to wonder whether these depots would still have closed if the **DaCSTaR** project was ongoing: probably not; housebuilding in Torrington and along the rail route south as far as Halwill Junction would have supported the Stibb Cross depot; new house building between Halwill Junction and Bude and on throughout North Cornwall would have supported the Bude depot.

Doing nothing as the oncoming recession takes its toll is the worst option. The announcement and implementation of a start to a programme such as **DaCSTaR** is the best possible alternative: it would boost the construction industry immeasurably in the localities of the 'lost' lines to be restored.

The ongoing works to improve 5 miles of the A361 North Devon Link Road just outside Barnstaple are costing £46,560,558 and have attracted a contractor from Abergavenny. Restoration of 250 miles of former railway lines within the peninsula would be budgeted in the region of £925 million and could conceivably benefit many and varied sized contractors from within the region. Furthermore, the restoration of stations and halts with access and car parking would also be work for local firms.

However, the greatest boom would be in house-building: 10,000 open-market homes and (at least) 10,000 affordable homes which are built over, say, 10 years and which are widely distributed throughout the peninsula will provide a sustained period of assured work for local builders, from large to small, building these 20,000 or more homes. The build costs are estimated at £160,000 (open-market) and £150,000 (affordable), both figures including infrastructure, which equates to a total £3.1 billion pounds (including expenditure on infrastructure and roads).

The social benefits of restoration: illustrations

Were all those 20,000 new homes to be distributed across only those four Devon Districts and the *former* North Cornwall District, within which most of the railway would be restored, the building programme might likely be in places condemned as excessive in such rural communities. Hence, a wider geographical area might be required, to include West Somerset District (many Exmoor villages would be served by the railway) and perhaps a wider area of Cornwall.

The 10,000 open-market homes would be sold with legally-binding restrictive covenants precluding their use as second-homes.

Of the 10,000 affordable homes, a percentage (say 50% or 5,000 homes) would be sold to indigenous residents of Devon and Cornwall, and these too would be sold with the same covenants. Additional covenants will preserve these homes as affordable in the future - *more on that later.*

The final proportion of affordable homes (5,000 or more) will be perpetuated indefinitely as long-term rental homes for the indigenous people of the region who have been evicted or who face eviction, and will remain under the control of the Housing Departments of Local Authorities.

The affordable housing result might be (for example):

- (North) Cornwall, North Devon, Torridge, Mid Devon, West Devon and West Somerset: 96% of the new housing stock, at 16% each; 1,600 affordable homes each (over 10 years), of which 800 would be sold and 800 would be within the control of each of the District Councils for allocation to rental tenants. Such a number would surely make a material difference to the social housing problem.

- The wider Cornwall 4%,

If the £100 million "social fund" were split (for example) 40% to local hospitals, 40% to social care (care homes *etc*) and 20% to miscellaneous costs within the Local Authority control, the benefits to each element would be:

£40 million to hospitals (£4m per annum)

£40 million to care homes (£4m per annum)

£20 million to other projects (£2m per annum)

Of course, were such a programme to succeed on this scale then it could be expanded and perpetuated, perhaps even indefinitely.

Downsides: are there any?

In the event of this restored network eventuating, there would be: an extensive railway network for public transport, 10,000 new affordable homes, 10,000 open-market new homes (all located close to access to the restored railway), a thriving environment for builders, for builders' merchants, one or more maintenance depots for rolling stock (and training opportunities for engineers), a massive public 'cohesion' or common community interest by virtue of the involvement of volunteers throughout the network, franchise establishments everywhere offering passenger services, a substantial boost throughout all the region of the network for accommodation providers.

But what if it does not work? What if there are insufficient (paying) passengers?

In the first instance, the frequency of train services could be reduced, as far as that might be demonstrated to be satisfactory.

In a worst-case scenario, the entire network would be closed to train operations.

What then?

The proposed capital funding solution provides for the entire cost to be met by the sale of 'premium' house plots to incomers to the two counties. Therefore, there has been no cost to any incumbent parties in Devon and Cornwall.

In fact (and assuming the whole of the 'lost' network has been restored), Local Authorities will have collectively benefited to the tune of £100 million (£10,000 x 10,000 open-market house plot sales).

10,000 affordable homes – *as a minimum* - will also have been built.

There would be a conversion of all restored lines to cycleways and footpaths, still providing an appealing attraction for tourists.

The metal of the rails would be taken up and sold.

In summary: there are no downsides to the project whatsoever.

The costs of restoration

The only information available to the author is the restoration cost for the Okehampton railway line to join the Tarka Line at Cheriton Bishop: it cost £40.5m (£10m under budget). Of the 14 miles which were upgraded, 11 miles of track were laid, with 24,000 concrete sleepers and 29,000 tons of ballast. This equates to, broadly stated, £3.7m per mile. This is rail restoration for a railway laid on an <u>existing</u> track-bed.

NB This is the physical cost of track laying and excludes all land acquisition costs including compensation to land owners. It also excludes the cost of stations and halts (and obviously rolling stock too).

Scrub clearance would add to that figure, but economies of scale for a network-wide restoration might conceivably be found to balance that.

As a first stage for rail restoration in the peninsula, the following towns are (in order of priority) candidates (and at £3.7m per mile):

Bideford could be reconnected to Barnstaple 9.5 miles, £35m

Tavistock (former North station) could be reconnected to Bere Alston 6 miles, £22.2m

and outside the **DaCSTaR** area of this document,

Helston could be reconnected to Gwinear Road on the mainline to Penzance 8 miles, £29.6m

As a second stage, the following towns are candidates:

Ilfracombe could be reconnected to Barnstaple* 15miles, £55.5m

* The former railway bridge crossing the River Taw alongside the Long (road) Bridge has long been demolished; however, a little way (a half-mile) upstream of the existing road bridge is another former railway bridge; could that be used to reinstate the link across the river? To do so, a new link would be required from the former Barnstaple Town to the former railway bridge, and this necessitates transiting the north end of the Long Bridge and transiting east through Rock Park, which is certainly an interesting prospect.

Outside the **DaCSTaR**-focused area of this document:

> **Brixham** could be reconnected to Churston: 2 miles, £7.4m
>
> **Sidmouth** could be reconnected to Feniton (Sidmouth Junction) on the mainline   8 miles, £29.6m
>
> None of these are inconceivable costs of impossible magnitude.

And as a third stage:

> **Bude** could be reconnected to Okehampton via Holsworthy and Halwill Junction   26 miles, £96.2 m
>
> **Padstow** could be reconnected to a (reconnected) Tavistock via Launceston (further improving rail connectivity for northern Cornwall):   56 miles,   £207.2m

How much rail track is there to restore?

The sum total of all the lost lines is about 250 miles.

Were the cost to be, broadly stated, about £3.7million per mile, it equates to £925 million.

As to the cost of the trains, the author has little information; however, the following snippet does provide an indication of magnitude:

"a bespoke fleet of 52 articulated metro-style **E**(electric)MUs for Merseyrail. The £460m fleet will replace the ex-BR Class 507/508 **EMUs** on the Merseyside 750V DC third-rail network from 2020."

> source: https://www.therailwayhub.co.uk/12310/moving-in-moving-on-moving-out/

The above trains referred to are relatively expensive (electric compared to diesel) urban, commuter trains and likely to be longer trains (more coaches) than what would be required for the rural lines considered by this paper. This rural network would require a fleet of at least 18 D(diesel)MU trains; on a pro-rata basis to the above electric ones, it indicates a capital cost of £159 million but might conceivably be considerably less because of the requirement for smaller, diesel-powered trains.

Additional costs (in simplistic terms) include: the cost of land appropriated, construction of station (platforms), safety fences where required, an operations HQ, a maintenance depot, fuelling provision, plus the additional costs associated with tourism-generators which the steam locomotive trains would be. These include coaling and watering facilities, and turntables. None of the above would seem, at face value, to represent costs approaching the magnitude of the two principal costs: (i) rail track (line) restoration and (ii) rolling stock.

In fact, the ongoing and extensive national replacement programme of older DMUs nationally would present the opportunity to buy older (used) rolling stock at bargain-basement prices, stock which still has a long life to offer on relatively slow branch lines.

This paper postulates capital receipts to fund the railway restoration from the share of house plot sales on the open market (at £110,000 per plot) and the sale of just 10,000 of such plots; the sum total of funds would be £1.1 **billion**. That would seem to be just about adequate; however, were there to be shortfall as the restoration program proceeded, the revenue-earning programme could be extended; thus, the programme completion can be assured; and the result is a restored branch railway network without the least debt burden.

The original budget for HS2 in 2015 was £55bn. The latest projected costs of HS2, a very doubtful scheme if ever there was one, are simply staggering; they exceed £156 billion*.

source: https://www.newcivilengineer.com/latest/dft-no-plans-to-cancel-hs2-despite-inflationary-cost-hike-claims-14-10-2022/#:~:text=Official%20costs%20for%20completion%20of,sits%20at%20%20%C2%A312.8bn.

That spend of £156bn on HS2 will get passengers (a tiny minority of the UK population) from Birmingham to London ten minutes faster. In fact, even that modest claim may prove to be untrue (at least until 2040!) because the line is now projected to terminate at Old Oak Common, well outside central London and necessitating a tube journey to reach even Euston Station.

Greenpeace claims that it would cost £55bn to insulate every UK home.

With energy costs sky-rocketing, with recession upon the economy, with inflation being the highest it has been for 40 years, which one is the wisest spend?

This **DaCSTaR** project, *i.e. purely the railway element,* were it funded by the state (which is <u>not</u> the foundation of the proposal herein), would cost just over £1 billion and would benefit all of the communities of northern Devon, North Cornwall and West Somerset, but the local government in these rural regions will undoubtedly perceive the prospects of gaining such a sum from central government funding as bleak; hence, the **DaCSTaR** mechanism and proposal recognises that.

What would be the cost of appropriating the necessary land in order to restore the lost <u>railway lines</u> to their original routes?

Such a question requires considerable research to quantify anything approaching an answer, and that is beyond the resources of the author. However, what can be said is that (a) the price offered to agricultural land owners would be close to agricultural value and not much more (perhaps double), and (b) the generation of cash from the related *sale* of open-market properties built on land purchased (*also at double agricultural value)* would far exceed the cost of necessary land to be bought for the railway line itself (excluding existing structures such as former railway stations converted to homes). It is not, therefore, a 'show stopper' but merits further consideration and a potential adjustment of outline budgets.

What other costs would be necessary?

The principal remaining cost would be resolving the conflicts between road and rail. Some former rail lines have been built on; the western section of the A361 North Devon Link Road is perhaps the largest example. It would necessitate some form of construction alongside the

Filleigh bridge - if the return of the road for that section to the 'old' road was (probably likely) deemed unacceptable. Many smaller new bridges everywhere would also be necessary, and (again) in simplistic terms these might be budgeted at a million pounds each.

Another example of road/rail conflict would be the Tiverton 'south bypass' road from the eastern outskirts to beyond the bridge over the River Exe to the west. It is beyond the scope of this paper to consider each and every one of such instances. However, what is feasible to consider in many instances such as this is to view the train as akin to a tram: running over the same route as vehicular traffic with conflicts potentially controlled by traffic lights. The train frequency is so light that such a resolution might well serve without the considerable expense of resorting to physical separation. Might this resolve the A361 conflict and the Filleigh bridge? It is an interesting subject to consider but (again) beyond the scope of this paper.

A brief and simplistic summary

The physical *restoration* of 250 miles of branch line railway track would cost about £925 million, the rolling stock might be about £100 million, a total of £1.025 billion. Allowing £75 million (broad brush) to cover the related miscellany makes a total of £1.1 billion *(perhaps therein the land cost for the railway lines might be found)*.

The restored network in totality includes more than 70 stations and halts. If the new homes were *equally* distributed around all these locations, it equates to 143 new homes in the region of each of them.

Such a building programme would be closely linked to the rail lines' restoration programme which would undoubtedly take a decade. This implies that 1,000 homes (open market) - plus 1,000 new (affordable) homes - per year would be built. This is not an unrealistic nor anything approaching an unattainable figure. It equates to 14 (open-market) plus 14 (affordable) new homes in (on average) each railway station or halt location each year for 10 years.

The population of the (whole of the) Devon and Cornwall peninsula is increasing at a rate of 1% per annum. Devon in 2020 had 1.2 million residents, Cornwall 570,000; the combined total for the peninsula is 1.77 million people. At an average occupancy of 2.36 persons per home, that equates to 750,000 homes. In all probability, the incoming 10% increase in the population of the peninsula *as a whole* over the next 10 years will be some 177,000 people (10%); and they will require 75,000 new homes (including within the major towns and cities).

The present population of the four Devon Districts (Torridge, North, West and Mid) and the former North Cornwall District is about 400,000 people. Their present housing stock is about 170,000 homes. On the same population growth numbers, over 10 years the population will increase by about 40,000 people and the number of homes by 17,000.

Adding 20,000 new homes to just these five Districts at the rate of 2,000 per year via the mechanism proposed represents almost 118% of the required additional housing stock in those five Districts. Such would seem to be monopolistic and locally excessive, and hence might be unlikely to go unchallenged by local housing developers.

However, the proposed, restored railway lines also extend into West Somerset to serve various Exmoor villages en route to Taunton; they extend very slightly into East Devon and thence to Exeter; and they extend also to Plymouth; in Cornwall the rail links via Bodmin will extend to the mainline and further south-west. In fact, there is relatively little in terms of area, region or District, which would not benefit from the restored railway lines.

Districts adjoining the 'northerly five' would be expected to take a share of the new homes to be built (open-market and affordable) and, similarly, share in the societal benefits.

The 20,000 new homes proposed by DaCSTaR represents about 27% per cent of the number that will be required throughout the whole peninsula over the next 10 years.

All these homes *and* those that already exist in proximity to the restored lines would enjoy rail access close at hand.

What kind of trains would suit? A return to steam?

In all the history of all trains within the British Isles, until very shortly before the Beeching closures decimated them, the steam locomotive was ubiquitous; for only a very few years before closure was the diesel locomotive introduced. Of course, the switch from steam to diesel could not have, by itself, transformed the dire operating economics such as to stave off closures; such was far beyond such economies offered by the transition from steam to diesel.

The diesel-hauled train *(and this document describes only passenger-carrying trains, freight being considered to be irretrievably lost)* was itself superseded by the diesel multiple unit or "DMU". **Diesel** being the propulsion; **Multiple** referring to the composition of the train in terms of number of **Units** (i.e. coaches; one coach only being the smallest train, a combined locomotive and coach). Historically, the steam locomotive-hauled train mandated complexity. Consider: the train arrived at its end-of-line or terminus with its coaches behind the locomotive. To exit the station by the same route (track), the locomotive had to be uncoupled from its train (of coaches) and then it had to return or "runround" said coaches on a parallel track before it could be re-coupled to its coaches at the other end of the train to depart the station. Worse: the locomotive (usually) had to be turned around 180 degrees before it was coupled to its coaches so that the locomotive 'faced' the route return (interesting exceptions existed on smaller trains on branch lines, but such is the province of history not of this document).

Hence, for steam-hauled trains, the station required at least two lengths of parallel track and a mechanism to turn around or reverse the direction of the steam locomotive; this was usually a turntable.

The substitution of diesel locomotives, which could drive either forwards or backwards (a driver's cab at each end) removed the need for a turntable, but the need for a parallel track (or runround 'loop' as it was called) remained.

Of course, many stations required more than one track and more than a single platform, and in such cases (with points *or switches* at each end of the station) one track could 'double' as the runround route for the locomotive.

The coming of the DMU removed the need for the "runaround" (track) loop. The DMU had a driver's cab at each end of the whole train. If it was a single unit (or coach) then that coach itself had a driver's cab at each end. Thus, the DMU could arrive and (without the least fuss or necessity for turning) depart in the opposite direction; it was therefore simple in operation and relatively inexpensive in track infrastructure. The DMU runs today on all branch lines and is the mandatory train format for restored lines; however, there is a caveat to this, and that is mandated by the potential purposes of such lines: the steam train is a powerful exception to the desirability of simplicity - *see below.*

Restoring lost railway lines with a view to minimisation of cost (of rebuilding and operation) and simplicity too of operation is facilitated by the DMU. This paper also initiates an exploration of how simple and to what maximum extent it might be possible to restore lost railways with single-track lines - *see below.*

Steam locomotives are something of a national passion, even today; many of them remain in (relatively occasional) service on minor lines or haul passenger trains on excursion 'specials' on main lines. However, they are unsuited to commuter train working. The locomotives require frequent loading of coal and water; they emit smoke - unpopular in urban environments. The driving of such locomotives is a technically-challenging task which requires considerable physical fortitude, most certainly so for the fireman, who has to shovel literally tons of coal for every few miles, and to do so in a punitively hot environment. Steam, for commuters, is therefore history.

However, steam for tourism has a very great potential indeed. The appeal is true also of niche market railways with diesel and electrical propulsion; consider: the Swiss 'Glacier Express' or the Australian 'Ghan', for example.

Steam-hauled trains have the potential to carry considerable numbers of tourists (else they would swiftly be discontinued). Properly marketed and managed, tourists might conceivably travel aboard a restored "**Atlantic Coast Express**" from, say, Taunton to Padstow, or on a "**Devon Belle**" from Plymouth to Ilfracombe, for example.

In each case, a longer train journey and to a seaside resort would bring tourist guests in significant numbers to patronise the hotels and

B&Bs of such resorts. Ilfracombe, for example, could benefit substantially.

The viability of restored 'lost' railway lines must be considered principally from the economic perspective: frequent services running to a stable timetable; yet, the steam-hauled drain for tourism can 'piggy-back' upon such restored lines with relatively little extra capital investment (principally in the above-mentioned "run-round" loop, where necessary, and in a turntable for the locomotive; coaling and watering facilities would also be required, but that is of much lesser capital cost).

Wales, for example, possesses three of the top ten most scenic railway lines in Europe, exceeding the appeal of even the scenic mountain railways of Switzerland, according to a survey by **Which?** The **Ffestiniog Railway**, the **Welsh Highland Railway** and the **Talyllyn Railway** are those three scenic railways, and all prosper despite their original promoters being dismissed as crackpots; in fact, in Wales there are now sixteen heritage railway lines, seven of them connected to the mainline. * Such railways bring many tourists.

The top 10 scenic railways in Europe according to Which? magazine:
1 Ffestiniog Railway, Wales
2 Bergen Railway, Norway
3 Bernina Express, Switzerland and Italy
4 Glacier Express, Switzerland
5 Brocken Railway, Germany
6 Talyllyn, Wales
7 Welsh Highland Railway, Wales
8 West Highland Line, Scotland
9 Flam Railway, Norway
10 Golden Pass, Switzerland

*source:
https://www.theguardian.com/travel/2022/sep/10/most-scenic-railway-in-europe-old-welsh-mining-line-became-a-world-beater-ffestiniog-wales

The spectacular sight of "6233 Duchess of Sutherland" topping Hemerdon; Penzance - Exeter St David's, 30th April 2022.

Photo: Bernard Mills.

Such trains as this would attract tens of thousands of tourists to the Devon and Cornwall peninsula.

It is quite a fascinating thought to consider a (probably *long* summer) schedule of many and varied steam trains operating on restored lines; offering excursions to incumbent residents from place to place and attracting tourists in volume to the region - bringing a reinvigoration to the traditional accommodation providers. Such services customarily offer a high standard of cuisine and service, creating employment for local people.

The appeal of the train, the sense of nostalgia for train trips, is widespread both in the UK and in foreign parts; so much so that a wide-ranging south-west network will undoubtedly appeal to tourists; indeed, the restoration of such famous train names of the past such as the **Atlantic Coast Express** and the **Devon Belle** could conceivably provide a bonanza of opportunities for the operators of restored lines and for the individual owners of tourist accommodation throughout the region.

As previously stated, the tiny, narrow-gauge Lynton steam railway attracts 40,000 passengers a year. It runs for only a mile, for which adult passengers pay £7.95 or (a family ticket) £19.95.

On a larger scale, the Swanage (steam) Railway (for example) carried 211,000 passengers last year and made an estimated £14m contribution to the local economy.

In Somerset the Minehead "Bluebell Line" railway is a success.

In South Devon, the Plym Valley heritage railway is similarly so.

In Launceston there is a narrow-gauge railway established on the former line to Padstow.

The Jacobite is a steam locomotive-hauled tourist train service that operates over part of the West Highland Line in Scotland. It has been operating under various names and with different operators every summer since as far back as 1984. It has played an important role in sustaining a scenic route.

The All Parliamentary Group on Heritage Rail in 2013 estimated that the then value of Britain's 100+ heritage railways was worth £250 million a year to the country.

Virgin Experience Days offers a wide portfolio of many and various steam excursions, some of which include overnight stays:

https://www.virginexperiencedays.co.uk/luxury-trains-and-heritage-steam

Indeed, there is now a plethora of steam-train excursions all over the UK; steam has been recognised as the popular attraction it truly is.

The tourist demand for steam trains is certainly there, and a network-wide opportunity to enjoy it would boost the appeal and economy of Devon and Cornwall by many millions of pounds each year; indeed, it is one more very valuable element of the **DaCSTaR** proposal.

Consider an "Atlantic Coast Express" train:

It might travel from Taunton (to attract tourists from 'Up Country') to Padstow (possibly the most celebrated tourist town in the south west after St. Ives).

The route would be a leisurely trip across Exmoor to Barnstaple (Junction) and thence along the *Atlantic* coast and the Torridge estuary to Bideford and the river to Torrington before venturing inland on the old Light Railway line to rural Halwill Junction; the train would then head south-west into Cornwall to Launceston; and, finally, follow the old North Cornwall Railway route to Wadebridge and along the Camel estuary to seaside Padstow.

The journey of 130 miles would take approximately 4 to 5 hours (at the envisaged 30 mph train speed of both yesteryear and restored railways). The tourist could then enjoy an afternoon and evening in Padstow (or two) and return the next day.

Doubtless great food would also be served in the train's restaurant coach. It is a marketing man's dream.

Steam locomotives would boost the appeal of such a 'tourist special' considerably.

Restored lines, stations and halts: a new, simpler format

Consider a restored 'simple' network structure like this: a train from A to B, a separate train from B to C, another train from C to D; all of them on dedicated tracks (with no interconnections) and hence offering relatively simple operational structures with lower costs: it is the safest system from the perspective of avoiding rail collisions.

Of course, this is, to a great extent, an over-simplification, but the principle is not to be dismissed lightly. The draft network structure proposal within this document aspires to this concept. Consider it akin to the London Tube where journeys from A to B to C *etc.* customarily mandate a change of train and (tube) line.

With apologies to the experienced railway infrastructure engineer, the following pages are written in simplistic terms for the benefit of others, people who will not have considered these factors but whose support will be needed if the proposals are ever to move towards implementation.

Simplicity is an aid to cost reduction in the general sense of every enterprise. In the case of railways, consider a line that runs from A to B **with a single train**; consequent to this simple arrangement, there is no need for passing places, for points (the rail industry may refer to them as 'switches') or signals (or signal boxes). Of course, this is an extremely simple example, but an adoption of it *in principle* would be very desirable. Indeed, it is feasible to adopt this principle of simplicity and to structure a new network of lines which hold to it with relatively few exceptions. In theory, the only persons employed requiring of technical skills might conceivably be only the train drivers: a corporate operating status which would be greatly beneficial for the minimisation of operating costs.

Of course, there will always be instances on single track railway lines where one train going east will meet another going west (for example). To avoid a head-on collision a passing place is necessary. In railway terminology such places are called 'passing loops'. In the past they were located at stations and the train going east would stop on the north side of the platform whilst the train going west would stop on the south side of the platform (of small rural stations); however, this meant that the platform would be 'surrounded' by the railway track, necessitating a footbridge.

Alternatively, there would be two platforms with the two railway lines running between them (and this was the norm); but pedestrian movement from one platform to the other still necessitated a footbridge. In today's world a footbridge with all its steps is deemed undesirable (and conceivably would also be illegal in discriminatory law). An alternative would be required.

In some cases, footbridges without steps but with ramps have been constructed in recent years to enable wheelchair users to cross roads (there is one such over the A39 approaching Barnstaple from the west), but these occupy a great deal of space - the gradient for a wheelchair necessitates a very long ramp indeed - and so they are expensive.

The maxim for this proposal for restoration of 'lost lines' is low cost simplicity; hence, alternative designs for all stations are considered.

In the past, the movement of trains over single-track lines was controlled by such crude devices as passing a token to the train driver before he ventured his train onto the single track. Waiting somewhere ahead of the train would be another train which could not proceed (in the opposite direction, i.e. converging) until the token was passed to the driver of that train, which necessitated the train with the token stopping so that the driver could hand it over. These days we have satellites and mobile-phone communication to aid management and minimise costs; but, more substantially, any new branch line could (at least in large part) be operated with the simple expedient of 'shuttling' from A to B and back, with onward journey to C (and further) aboard a second 'shuttle', such that each line was worked by only a solitary train, removing all requirement for signals and for points operation; the highest level of safety being assured by virtue of there being only a single train ever on every section of track. With few exceptions, this is the arrangement postulated. For new stations and halts, footbridges are out (wheelchair-unfriendly) and so are subways (cost); so, alternatives of design are required.

Historical station (platform) layouts:

Opposite page:

Figure One: A simple 'halt' on a single-track line will have one platform on one side of the track, and trains going both ways (if and when a restored line graduates to two trains running) will both stop for pedestrians to access the same platform. It presupposes that car parking will be on that side of the railway line. In such a case, there is no requirement for pedestrians to cross the track. The implication is that the east-bound train (to continue the example) will pass the west-bound train *somewhere else*, somewhere outside the station.

Figure Two illustrates the access problem if trains were to pass (each other) within the station and with a platform within the 'passing loop'. Of course, the two tracks could be located alongside each other on one side of the platform, but that is inherently undesirable because it prevents either the east-bound or the west-bound passengers accessing the train as their train never comes alongside the platform.

Figure Three: Historically, these access difficulties were resolved with scant thought for disabled persons in wheelchairs and with the construction of a footbridge or:

Figure Four: in larger stations where more expense could be justified, an underground tunnel or subway could be built to permit pedestrian travel to all platforms. However, such an expense could not be contemplated for the restoration of the 'lost lines'.

Historical station (platform) layouts:

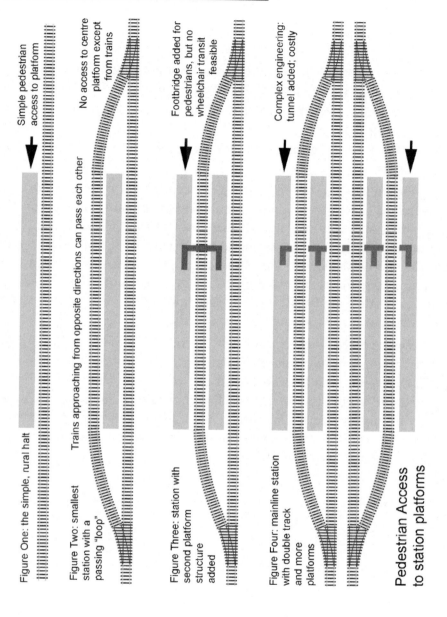

Simple pedestrian access to platform

No access to centre platform except from trains

Footbridge added for pedestrians, but no wheelchair transit feasible

Complex engineering: tunnel added; costly

Figure One: the simple, rural halt

Trains approaching from opposite directions can pass each other

Figure Two: smallest station with a passing "loop"

Figure Three: station with second platform structure added

Figure Four: mainline station with double track and more platforms

Pedestrian Access to station platforms

Alternative station (platform) layouts:

Opposite page:

Figure Five (is Fig. One again): the simple single-line halt remains valid. Passengers may board or alight at trains going either east or west.

Figure Six (is similar to Fig. Two): the passing loop remains but it is relocated elsewhere, <u>outside the station</u>. Trains will pass each other where there is no requirement for pedestrians to conflict with train movements.

Figure Seven: this illustrates a second platform structure with pedestrians able to move between the two because the second line *terminates* and only one line *transits* the station. It is ideally suited to instances where one line terminates. Of course, if both trains are to transit east-west or west-east then one will have to reverse out of the terminus to gain the transit line; this is not ideal but on a rural railway with very little train traffic it is no great imposition for the modern DMU train which can run forwards or backwards.

Figure Eight: this is, essentially, a more complex version of Figure Seven: a substantial number of platforms exist to serve multiple lines but only one line is a true east-west *or transit* line; all other trains must reverse and switch to the 'transit' line if required. Such a configuration would be unlikely to be favoured for a busy urban station, but that is not the situation in the case of the lost lines, which are generally rural in character and with low traffic.

Alternative station (platform) layouts:

Alternative station platform structures

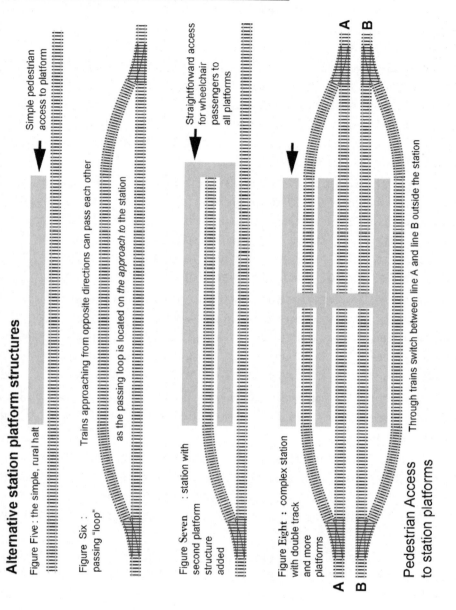

Figure Five : the simple, rural halt

Simple pedestrian access to platform

Figure Six : passing "loop"

Trains approaching from opposite directions can pass each other

as the passing loop is located on *the approach to* the station

Figure Seven : station with second platform structure added

Straightforward access for wheelchair passengers to all platforms

Figure Eight : complex station with double track and more platforms

A

B

A

B

Pedestrian Access to station platforms

Through trains switch between line A and line B outside the station

In historical operation on branch lines the passengers were allowed to walk across the track to reach the opposite platform; such as called a 'barrow crossing' because the incumbent station staff would transfer goods and materials such as post and baggage across the track in a wheelbarrow. In the context of restored, single line, branch railway stations it is still a perfectly sound concept: it allows for wheelchairs to cross without a footbridge. Furthermore, train speeds in such stations would be extremely slow, barrow crossing lights would flash to alert pedestrians of an approaching train, and the train driver would also resort to a klaxon, a loud one.

Most stations and halts on a restored network would require no more than a Figure One/Five single platform serving trains passing in both directions (the necessary passing loop would be remote from the station). Essentially, this works because passengers do not get off the eastbound train (for example) in order to board the westbound train. Passengers either board from the platform or alight from the train.

Where train line junctions exist and passengers require to change trains/lines, and where one train might wait for an arrival on another line, two train tracks are required. A Figure Two construction - with a barrow crossing - could serve, or a Figure Seven construction also serves if the station is the terminus for one of the two lines.

With a high priority on minimisation of capital costs in rebuilding stations, the 'barrow crossing' would be at the forefront of design considerations.

In fact, in northern Devon (for example) there would be only two significant instances of a relatively more complex station structure being required; these are Barnstaple, which would revert to its historical name in the railway heyday (Barnstaple *Junction*) and Halwill Junction.

In the case of Barnstaple, it is a station constrained by its urban geography; but, fortunately, the requisite additional platform is already there, intact, and could be relatively easily restored. See the following graphic design for a rekindled, pedestrian-friendly Barnstaple Junction station which needs no footbridge restoration.

Proposed railway lines and platforms at Barnstaple Junction:

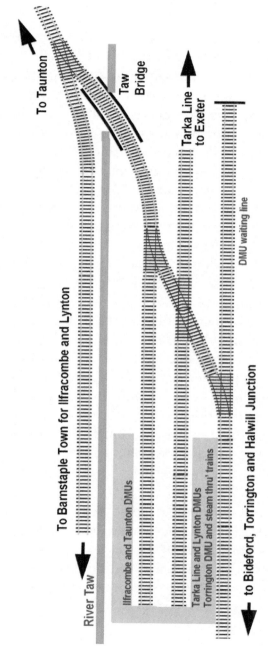

A revitalised Barnstaple Junction would be the hub for trains from Ilfracombe, from Lynton, from Taunton, from Bideford (and Torrington to the south of it) and, of course, for the existing Tarka Line connection to Exeter.

The network schema accommodates all these lines. In the case of the first three lines the access for trains to the station is via the existing bridge over the River Taw approximately a mile to the east.

The obvious question is: How could Ilfracombe and Lynton trains actually reach and cross that bridge? In the initial stages trains from both towns would enter Barnstaple's urban environment on the old lines restored to reach a restored Barnstaple Town station on the north bank of the River Taw. In the case of the Lynton line a traffic light arrangement would be necessary to halt vehicular traffic to allow the train to transit today's existing roads. Significantly, no substantive changes would be required for those roads. At that location, the train must be considered as akin to an urban 'tram' - with one difference: the train track, except for where it actually crosses the roads in the Pilton / River Yeo bank location, does not require insetting into the road surface; rather, it passes along the (very quiet, traffic restricted) North Walk, Castle Street and the Strand to reach and cross the Clock Tower square (after crossing the Old Bridge road via traffic lights) and continuing along the Taw Vale riverfront to and through the park and ultimately to gain a junction north of the river bridge with the restored Taunton line. But this is to delve into detail, likely contentious detail; and so the outline description, simplistic as it must be at this stage, is included solely to provide a basis for consideration of a comprehensively restored railway line to both Ilfracombe and Lynton which would connect with other lines located on the south side of the River Taw.

The River Yeo swingbridge would likely also require replacement; boat access to the Pilton Quay might be brought to an end. These changes must be considered in the context of the benefits to the very many more people of Ilfracombe, Lynton and Barnstaple. How many times does the Yeo swingbridge actually open in any year?

One further aspect of Barnstaple Junction merits mention: an **"Atlantic Coast Express"** steam train (from Taunton and heading for Padstow) would transit the station via the Taw bridge and continue satisfactorily, but a steam-drawn train passing through Barnstaple from the south and over the Taw bridge to Ilfracombe would require a turntable to turn its locomotive.

In fact, the draw of steam locomotives hauling tourist 'specials' or even timetabled excursion trains adds a level of complexity (and cost) to the necessary track infrastructure.

Steam locomotives go forwards pulling their carriages, and don't usually go backwards pushing their train carriages. A short train basis (one carriage) did actually do this before the arrival of the DMU, the "autotrain", but it is not a basis for the future for restoration of steam locomotive specials travelling a greater distance.

Hence, turntables would be required at all terminus stations used by steam locomotives; such would include: Padstow, Ilfracombe, Okehampton, Barnstaple (possibly on the north bank of the River Taw beyond the bridge), Marsh Mills, Bude and Halwill Junction.

The author inclines to the view that the capital cost of turntables would be far outweighed by the commercial benefit from the very substantial appeal of steam trains and the tourist spend that they would draw.

The challenge is to identify the suitable location for a turntable in each case, potentially in locations adjacent to 'lost lines' which have subsequently been developed.

In the case of terminus stations, it might be the case that new or substitute stations may necessitate being constructed further out of town. This might also offer greater opportunities for car parking; no bad thing for many railway users; a bus service between town centres and railway stations may well prove to be a requisite component of a network restoration.

Proposed railway lines and platforms at a new Halwill Junction station:

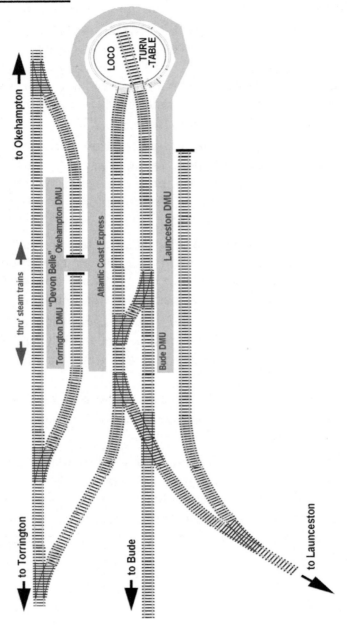

The second junction of significance for an inter-connected railway lines system in the region would be **Halwill Junction**.

Formerly, the lines from Torrington, Bude, Launceston and Okehampton conjoined at Halwill Junction. Nothing whatsoever of it exists today; indeed, the station approach for thr three lines (other than the Okehampton one) has been built on; a small housing estate is there.

However, the three aforementioned lines (Okehampton excepted) all approached from the north and were very close together. That location, where they formerly converged, which is north of the housing estate, would seem to be a suitable location for a new Halwill Junction station; it would be just north of the northenmost house in Beeching Close and just west of that house on the opposite side of Chilla Road.

It leaves only the onward or transit line to Okehampton to find its sinuous, snaking path through the hamlet to gain the historical track to the south, to Okehampton ultimately, and there to connect with the newly-restored train connection to Exeter. The route from a new Halwill Junction station would be to cross the Chilla Road and across the field immediately east of Chilla Road, to cross Draybury Lane just east of that house which is east of the Winsford Trust building, to cross the field behind and east of the primary school and so to gain the old track-bed to Okehampton.

Fortunately, such a new station would have only this one transit line (North to South, to Okehampton) and the three terminus stations serving Launceston, Bude and Torrington; which would afford scope to adopt one of the 'alternative' station designs aforementioned.

The Halwill Junction design also includes a locomotive turntable which would enable the operation of 'tourist trains' including ones hauled by diesel and steam locomotives, which could be turned about to 'run round' their train to haul it in the out (of the terminus) direction and on towards an ultimate destination such as Padstow for a restored "Atlantic Coast Express".

Essential and desirable station services:

Walking or cycling to gain access to a station and train will always be perceived as laudable, but it is not an option for many people who are incapable of such physical activity: the infirm, the elderly and the disabled; nor, indeed, does it appeal to the lazy; but the train aspires to serve everyone, as far as it is possible to do so.

Car parking is essential for more rural stations and halts in order to accommodate the conjunction of the car and the train. Not providing a car park is the greatest deterrent to switching to the train.

In more urban locations which serve commuters it may be perceived as less than essential: commuters arrive and depart by train.

All stations/halts must offer toilets, clean ones which are not off-putting. The local Parish Council could and might well assume responsibility for some station services including the maintenance of toilets; alternatively, the employment of a far-ranging (could it be mobile by virtue of the train?) toilet maintenance service is another option, a job-creating one.

Coffee and sandwiches *etc* availability would be desirable; certainly, at those stations where passengers would have to wait for a train inter-connection. These services could be franchised out, the awarding of the franchise possibly under the control of the Parish Council. For the same reasons of infrequency, the natire of the service at the most rural halts would not be hugely profitable, and so might be a local volunteer service.

Station cleaning, litter removal, waste bins emptying *etc*. These are most likely either local volunteers or perhaps more likely a far-ranging mobile contractor (could it be mobile by virtue of the train?) more job-creation.

Basic weather shelter is essential for anyone waiting for a train, and with seating. The dismaying question of vandalism is one that will have to be considered. Sadly, there is always likely to be an inconsiderate minority of cerebrally-challenged people, and so all station facilities (many of which stations will be unmanned halts) must be designed with the prospect of vandalism in mind.

This probably means hard seats, indestructible plastic ones. It also means that both toilets and shelters must be designed or monitored to preclude them becoming overnight places of shelter for the homeless. Again, this raises the desirability of having the most local participation - such as the Parish Council might undertake - to lock and unlock such facilities as required.

As even the most remote halt would have at least a shelter from the weather, the roof could be covered with electricity-generating solar-panels, charging a battery; the battery could energise platform lights in the late-afternoon and also power a CCTV, triggered by infra-red / movement detection; if necessary an alarm signal and video capture could also be sent to a Parish guardian, and such a person could conceivably also be a Special Constable for the British Transport Police.

Vending machines may be a useful service on those stations where an assured presence of passengers can deter criminal abuse. However, the proposed network restoration is essentially one of prevalently minor stations and rural halts, places which necessitate either nil or the most minimal of services delivered by people; the station is where the train is boarded or exited; it does not need or aspire to be more, save for the avoidance of discomfort for waiting passengers: the network is the train, the journey; the convenience is being aboard the train, not the station.

All stations and halts should offer a rain-sheltered and secure opportunity to secure a bicycle before boarding a train; this must be secure from theft; something akin to a 'micro-shed' (perhaps the cyclist might apply his/her own padlock) or, at least, the familiar steel 'hoops' fixed to the floor.

It hardly needs mentioning, but all platforms must be wheelchair-friendly; this includes the aforementioned 'barrow crossing' where necessary.

Stations and halts would provide network information, timetables *etc*. They could also provide paid advertising opportunities (local attractions for example).

Finally (at least for the moment), stations should ideally provide free wifi for the waiting passengers.

The costs of operation: How could such be affordable?

The principle of parsimony (or "Ockham's Razor") might well have been created for the operation of rural railway lines; it states that **"entities should not be multiplied beyond necessity"**. More familiar to many people is the "KISS" acronym or *"Keep it simple, stupid"*. More illustrious personages also quoted the concept:

Leonardo da Vinci	*"Simplicity is the ultimate sophistication";*
Shakespeare	*"Brevity is the soul of wit";*
Mies van der Rohe	*"Less is more".*

In considering railway line restoration and the ultimate costs of operation in order to determine and control costs so as to strive for sustained viability, the principle is an excellent starting point. It is also valuable from a safety perspective.

Lack of patronage (and costs far in excess of receipts) doomed the former branch lines to closure, and this was in those days when wages were (in real terms) relatively less than they are today. Even minor branch stations employed at least two staff, and there were signal box men and others; together that represents an expensive and unsustainable wage bill for any future prospects of viable operation.

Volunteers hold an appeal, certainly; but without employment contracts the availability, as and when required, of essential staff is not assured. Volunteers can be looked to for day-to-day, *less critical* tasks such as station maintenance and services; however, they cannot be expected to drive trains.

The author envisages community participation as essential for the rekindling and sustainability of rail services, to the extent that some form of 'adoption' of stations and halts within each Parish would be a highly desirable if not essential, fundamental principle of operations. Every community would benefit from local railway access; and every Parish council (the broad representative of all the communities within the District or County) should be encouraged, even incentivised, to participate. Such incentives might include: a say in train scheduling to meet particular local needs; perhaps participation in the location of the open-market and affordable housing; the operation of any link bus service associated with stations and halts *etc.*

The Parishes might also contribute the conductor / guards for the trains in the form of volunteers, incentivised by free rail trail; indeed, being a 'rail ranger' within a community could conceivably be appealing.

Ownership: Who would own the lines?

The UK railways were privatised in 1997. Recent years have demonstrated the downside of and the significant impediments to the operation of a UK railway where the track is owned by one party (Network Rail), the trains (since 1994) by another (various leasing companies) and the train operation by various *further* parties, franchisees. This "multiple parties and inherent conflicts of interest" has resulted in the operation of several lines being renationalised. The fortunes of the several franchisees has been mixed.

The following information is courtesy of Wikipedia:

"Currently five rail franchises are under public ownership (effectively they are nationalised):

LNER, **Northern Trains** and **Southeastern** are operators of last resort owned by the Department for Transport;

Transport for Wales Rail is owned by Transport for Wales, a Welsh-Government owned company, with no current plans to re-privatise the latter.

On 1 April 2022, **ScotRail** was put under public ownership by the Scottish Government, under Transport Scotland as **ScotRail Trains** operating on the same day.

During 2020, in the midst of the COVID-19 pandemic, all train operating companies (TOCs) entered into emergency measures agreements (EMAs) with the UK and Scottish Governments. Normal franchise mechanisms have been amended, transferring almost all revenue and cost risk to the government, effectively 'renationalising' the network temporarily.

In September 2020, the Government permanently got rid of the rail franchising system.

On 20th May 2021, the Government announced a white paper that would transform the operation of the railways. The rail network will be partly renationalised, with infrastructure and operations brought together under the state-owned public body Great British Railways. Operations will be managed on a concessions model.

On 18th November 2021, the government announced the biggest ever public investment in Britain's rail network, costing £96 billion and promising quicker and more frequent rail connections in the North and Midlands.

The so-called Integrated Rail Plan (IRP) includes substantially improved connections North-South as well as East-West and includes three new High Speed Lines."

source: Wikipedia

https://en.wikipedia.org/wiki/Rail_transport_in_Great_Britain#:~: text=Currently%20five%20franchises%20are%20under,owned%20comp any%2C%20with%20no%20current

use licensed under: https://creativecommons.org/licenses/by-sa/3.0/

In contrast to the failed franchises (above) the west coast main line franchise has proven to be a lucrative one; it was awarded initially to Virgin Rail but in August 2019 the franchise was taken over by a consortium of First Group and the Italian state rail operator, Trenitalia.

That franchise (and line) is only one of the UK railway lines which have been taken over by foreign state rail operators. The German state railway, Deutsche Bahn, controls four, including the London overground and the Grand Central line to Sunderland.

Several lines are controlled by the Dutch state railway, Nederlandse Spoorwegen (NS); these include: Merseyrail and the West Midlands Railway. Other railways are operated by the French state railway, SNCF, including the Thameslink. Very few UK railways are now owned and operated by UK companies.

This contrasts dramatically with the original objective of privatisation: to introduce competition, thereby lowering prices and improving services; but those aspirations could hardly stand up to a reality check: each line was effectively a monopoly in its area of operations. The lack of success, evident in lines which have been renationalised, is a stark warning to any aspirant railway owner or operator: the enduring preference for car travel is a tough nut to crack;

indeed, those lines that have succeeded, such as the West Coast line has done so by virtue of its long distance advantage over the car.

The fractured disarray of separate ownership of rail stock, rail lines and the fundamental short-termism of franchising have all militated against investment. In short, it is hard to see that such a construction of different interests could ever have succeeded; at least for most lines.

One undesirable result is that UK ticket prices have risen and are now expensive relative to other countries.

Whilst the UK splintered its national railway network into disparate, regional monopolies, this did not happen in Europe. The result has been that smaller UK franchisees have been taken over by the state-owned railway companies of other, major EU countries.

A perceptive and illuminating article in The Guardian of 10th January 2022 makes for fascinating reading:

https://www.theguardian.com/commentisfree/2022/jan/10/uk-railways-nationalise   *Christian Wolmar*

Copyright and licensing considerations preclude verbatim reproduction, but **the most important points are as follows**:

- Franchising has failed and that approach to train operating has been scrapped, and now only management contracts are awarded - effectively a renationalisation in all but name

- Rail services are at substantial risk of deteriorating to the extent of similar declines of fifty years ago;

- There is a prospect that fare rises, overcrowded trains and fewer services (which the Department for Transport is considering) will encourage a reversion to the car;

- Objective reflection illustrates that the British Rail of the past was Europe's most efficient railway;

- A good railway aids the prosperity of those towns it serves, and towns without one decline;

- Railways are part of the essential fabric of the country, a catalyst for prosperity; *and finally, an interesting point:*

- No one questions the sense of preserving B-**roads** with near-nil traffic.

The full article is well worth reading.

An objective analysis of the events of recent years - such as the Guardian article by Christian Wolmar - might conclude that some form of state ownership represents the only viable method for operation and maintenance of railway lines; indeed, a more defined conclusion might be that the ownership of the track (and track-bed including the stations), the rolling stock and the operations should best be consolidated within a single party, a new **British Rail**.

In considering rail line restorations, the elephant in the room is, of course: *Who will finance the considerable capital investment?*

Therein lies the key question: is it even possible that the financiers, the titular owners of the infrastructure *and* the rolling stock and the train operators could or should be the same party? That is far from the case today.

Of course, the government could be such a singular party; the government could be financier; in doing so, the government could be the owner; but the government has a reluctance to be an operator; and the franchise system of relatively recent years has demonstrated that it is fragile and will not sustain operational losses such that - *before long* - some form of intervention becomes necessary; and that, of course, usually means the state.

All of the above suggest that a more unorthodox approach to ownership and operation is worth consideration, perhaps even necessitated; even a radically different one.

In considering this prospect for unorthodoxy it is necessary to examine the purpose of any restored railway line and to identify the benefits and beneficiaries of it. These would include local people, local businesses (particularly the hospitality sector) and tourists; that these beneficiaries are both *local* to the restored railways and (to tourists) *from further afield* makes it a more complex question to consider.

Furthermore, a railway line in isolation is greatly disadvantaged compared to one which is linked to a network, local and national.

In short, the assured and titular owner of a railway *line* (both track-bed and stations) would appear to be the owner *of last resort*, i.e. the government (national, regional or more local); and that has been the case since the 1948 nationalisation for all railways which have operated since (with the exception of minor and relatively short lines of what are, essentially, tourist attractions).

With the major conclusion drawn that the track-bed of significant (longer) railway lines *to be restored* should be either the state (see elsewhere within this paper the mechanism for re-acquisition by the state of sold-off former track-bed and stations) or, alternatively, another form of public owner, the second consideration is the financing of restoration. That particular question is closely followed by:

Who will actually pay for the operational costs after restoration?

If there were to be any element of corporate borrowing with either some form of interest and repayment charges to private enterprise lenders or to the state, therein lies a potentially difficult overhead for the restored network operator. Given that the operational success of any restored railway line can only be estimated at the outset and the accuracy of any estimates will come with a relatively wide range of possibilities, any private sector loan finance must be expected to come with a significant interest premium; furthermore, if the freehold land title rests with the state then the security for any private sector loan finance for infrastructure capital costs is, to some degree, uncertain. These factors, ultimately, necessitate that a public body (in some form, possibly including regional and even local government) must be the financier of restoration.

Large scale developments of other kinds, housing in particular, have associated obligations put upon the private sector developer (in the form of Section 106 Agreements) and which may place the developer under a financial obligation to contribute to local public investment, including infrastructure projects.

Indeed, a Section 106 agreement has been imposed on a developer in North Devon, building 250 homes in Fremington. Seemingly, a levy is intended to build 11 homes for local people. *

* source: https://www.northdevongazette.co.uk/devon-cpre-welcomes-affordable-homes-for-fremington-using-developer-cash/

The crucial point is that such impositions upon, and such contributions from, developers of *private* sector houses are demonstrably an accepted *modus operandi* for raising the funds for *public* sector housing; and that is the key ingredient for the author's proposal (*with significant differences*).

There is no reason why an expansion in such an approach could not be used to create *affordable* homes *for sale* to *local* people, some of whom may be homeless.

It would seem, therefore, that in evaluating and preparing any proposal for rail line restoration that the possibilities for compulsory private sector contributions should be considered to a great degree; indeed, they are postulated as the primary source of funding for the capital costs of restoring the whole rail network of 'lost' lines.

Of course, this is a potentially sensitive subject in the wider consideration of affordability of new homes, particularly so for first-time buyers; yet a restored and widespread rail network would offer compensatory benefits to many such buyers: travel to and from place of employment and to shops *etc* without the cost of a motor car.

Accepting then that the freehold title to the infrastructure belongs to the state (most likely the national government but potentially more local government) and the cost of restoration are both within the ambit of the state (in whichever level of state the restoration costs might be found, generated and incurred), that leaves the question of the operation of the railway line(s).

Lines in the plural, because the wide geographical distribution of them (even within the regional **DaCSTaR** evaluation) suggests the possible or perhaps even likely prospect of there being more than one operator. *Who should they be? Who are the interested parties?*

In considering this question, the failure and termination of larger scale rail franchises in recent years weighs heavily against the private sector; hence, it leaves (once more) only the state; however, the state in this more localised context also includes local government: County, District, and perhaps even Parish.

The District Council for Ilfracombe (to return to the previous example) would be keen to see the enduring benefits of a rail line (the benefits are detailed elsewhere in this document); so might be the Town or Parish Council representatives, the Ward Members; indeed, Devon County Council too would be a party with a particular interest in the success and sustainability of such a rail link within its ambit, and with a wider focus on continuing its connectivity with other railway lines within and across the county and which link to Cornwall and Somerset too (with main line links).

Hence, were the more local councils (even Parish ones) to be associated with the *operation* of restored railway lines (at a level which they were able to determine and at which they were comfortable with) then the acute question is, unavoidably, how to maintain that association, even management, without exposure to the risk of operational losses, which local government can neither justify nor afford, particularly so as it would seem that more difficult economic times lie ahead at the time of writing; indeed, such weak economic prospects might logically doom any proposal for rail restoration to only the most cursory glance and rapid rejection. But that is pessimistic, and any reader of this proposal more likely possesses a degree of interest which, if not optimistic, might be considered constructive.

All potentially interested parties and their participation can be considered: Local government at the County and District level has no financial 'surplus' to devote to a project of this character or unknown prospects. Similarly, Parish councils have no funding at all.

This paper proposes a mechanism for the funding of construction, one which will also alleviate the affordable homes crisis and also boost local government coffers generally; however, all of that can be - and probably should be - disassociated from ultimate ownership of the land and physical infrastructure of the restored railway.

In fact, to preserve the integrity of the restored network for times to come, it would seem that ownership of the land and infrastructure should be held by a non-governmental organisation, one which could not be subjected to financial pressures beyond its control and the inherent risk of loss of such assets.

The above suggests that assets should be owned by a charitable or non-profit organisation, one with no borrowings whatsoever.

Such a body (let us call it the "Network Owner") would require operational funding to cover at least a modicum of administrative costs, but these would be relatively small and funded from ongoing contributions from the capital proceeds of the (indefinitely) continuing open-market house plot sales.

The rolling stock, bought from the capital proceeds of the open-market house plot sales (£110,000 contribution per each of 10,000 houses) should also be owned by the Network Owner.

Network (line) maintenance would be subcontracted to private sector companies on an individual line basis. The performance monitoring of such companies would be carried out by the representatives of the Parish Councils through whose 'patch' the line and trains ran; thence reported to the administrative function of the Network Owner.

Stations and halts would - to the maximum possible extent - be managed by volunteers sourced from within the Parishes through which the line and trains run; a minimum cost approach.

Train drivers (and possibly/probably) guards would be employed by a private company owned by the Network Owner. This company would also operate the trains. It would be funded from travel (ticket) receipts, with any deficit covered by the capital proceeds of the (indefinitely) continuing open-market house plot sales. As such, the annual capital receipts - were they sustained at the rate of (say) a mere 100 homes per year - would attain £11 million p.a. Were more to be required, in the case of an operational deficit, the volume of house sales could be increased.

The above exposes the network to two risks: (1) the operational costs exceeding the ticket sales and, in such a case, (2) a housing sale crisis resulting in an inability to subsidise losses from house sales' receipts (£110k per house).

There is no certainty, and nor can there ever be, for any enterprise which incurs costs and is therefore exposed to ultimate insolvency; however, the above platform: a restored network with no structural borrowing and a fallback, if necessary, on income from a proven resource (house sales) would put the restored network in a stronger position than other, conventionally-financed, railways.

The proposed *modus operandi* allows for (indeed, it requires) the most local of contribution at the lowest level: i.e. the Parish. It provides an incentive for the most local population to take an interest in its prospects, its operation, and to participate to the maximum *local* extent. Indeed, within the operational management structure of the restored network it would seem inherently desirable to have a committee of Parish representatives which could discuss and debate those operational aspects which might arise from time to time.

There is an important necessity for liaison with District Councils and with Cornwall County Council in the location, generation and granting of planning permissions for new homes.

There is a requirement for a body to manage the purchase and appropriation of the necessary land for the restored lines and stations *etc*.

The nature and structure of these bodies and mechanisms warrants detailed considerations beyond the preliminary nature of this paper.

In summary:

(i) the purchased freehold of all track-bed, stations and halts would belong to (the Network Owner) a charitable body, **a charitable Trust**; let's call it **Devon and Cornwall Sustainable Trains and Railways ("DaCSTaR")**;

(ii) the (many and varied, local) Trustees would be one person appointed from each Parish Council;

(iii) the Management or Executive Board would be (say) fifteen or more persons elected from all the Parish Councils' appointed representatives.

Such a structure means that there would be a desirable ownership and (importantly) management separation between **Devon and Cornwall Sustainable Trains and Railways ("DaCSTaR")** Executive Board and the County and District Councils.

The Executive Board personnel would have delegated functions, including such as:

1. Liaison with County and District Councils on the subject of permission for and siting of open-market and affordable homes;
2. Sales of plots (via local estate agents) for open-market homes;
3. Tendering for appointments of building contractors for affordable homes;
4. Building affordable homes;
5. Appropriation of necessary land for railways lines and stations including car parking;
6. Tendering for an appointment of building contractors for railway track-bed route clearance, stations and halts *etc*;
7. Monitoring of contractors in all endeavours;
8. Financial control;
9. Purchase of rolling stock;
10. Tendering for the operation of station franchises and the monitoring thereof;
11. Scheduling of trains, timetables;
12. Preservation and construction of walking/cycling trails;
13. Personnel management (of train drivers and guards); and a
14. Managing Director

Conceivably there could be an incentive (possibly collective) financial remuneration package for members of the Executive Board; such might include:

- £1,000 (*for example*; doubtless such sums would likely be higher) **for every open-market house plot sold** (plots would be sold; the Trust would not build the homes, that is for the free market and local builder);

- £1,000 for **every affordable home built**;
- £1,000 for **every mile of railway track built**; *etc*

The preservation of existing (and potentially future) walking & cycling trails

It's essential that the greatly-valued opportunities for walkers and cyclists on such as the Tarka and Camel Trails are maintained; indeed, the restoration of railway lines should offer the opportunity to enhance walking and cycling by virtue of providing drop-off and pick-up points all over a restored network without the necessity to use cars to gain access in the first instance.

In this respect, cycles should be housed within the brake van of the traditional train format ("consist" in railway terminology) as hauled by steam and diesel locomotives, but also provision should be made within the commuter DMUs which offer a frequent service on all lines.

How can the existing trails be preserved when the train line is restored on the track-bed?

Avon Valley Railway, Bitton. Photo: Bernard Mills.

Co-existence between every restored railway and established walking trails is an essential pre-requisite if popular support is to be secured.

Single-line railways are narrow. In many but not all instances, the historical track-bed provided for two parallel rail tracks; such width as that offers scope for maintaining the *status quo* of the paths and cycling trails. Where, as was the case in many instances, the historical rail line was only single-track, such extensive clearance of scrub growth, the laying of sleepers, metal rails *etc* will require heavy machinery - excavators and suchlike. It will be no great challenge for such machines to clear the necessary parallel track for the 'lightweight' pedestrians and cyclists whilst restoring the railway track-bed - which takes priority for the train, being heavier.

Importantly, in the case of other 'lost' railway lines which have never enjoyed a walking/cycling trail, it would be feasible to create one alongside the restored railway, much enhancing the choice and opportunity for walkers and cyclists in many other locations, all served by the railway to transport them to start and end points.

The legal necessities and the Law: an Enabling mechanism

The right for Local Authorities to appropriate land is enshrined within several mechanisms of UK law:

The Town and Country Planning Act 1990, Section 226 confers such powers:

"**226** Compulsory acquisition of land for development and other planning purposes.

(1) A local authority to whom this section applies shall, on being authorised to do so by the Secretary of State, have power to acquire compulsorily any land in their area:

> (a) if the authority think that the acquisition will facilitate the carrying out of development, re-development or improvement on or in relation to the land,

> (b) which is required for a purpose which it is necessary to achieve in the interests of the proper planning of an area in which the land is situated."

However, there is a caveat which militates against this mechanism: (i) the land must <u>already have planning permission</u> (for houses in this case) and (ii) compensation must be paid to the owner.

As the purposes of appropriation of land is (in part, *the other part being railway track-bed*) to fund the housing element of the project from the 'gained value' of <u>subsequently</u> granting the planning permission for housing, any financial benefit for the project would be unachievable as that value would pass to the owner of the land being appropriated as compensation.

Hence this Act may be only of limited or, most likely, even nil suitability.

The Transport and Works Act 1992

The original 19th century railways were approved by Parliamentary Railway Acts. However, since 1992, an order made under the Transport and Works Act 1992 (the TWA) is the usual way of authorising a new railway or tramway scheme in England and Wales today, except for nationally significant rail schemes in England which require development consent under the Planning Act 2008.

https://www.gov.uk/government/publications/transport-and-works-act-orders-a-brief-guide-2006/transport-and-works-act-orders-a-brief-guide

"Orders under the Transport and Works Act 1992 ("the TWA 1992") can authorise guided transport schemes and certain other types of infrastructure project in England and Wales.

Promoters of schemes of this kind often need a range of powers to put their scheme into practice. Under the TWA 1992, a promoter can apply to the Secretary of State for an order giving those powers. The order, if made, is known as a TWA order.

The powers that can be given in a TWA order can be very wide-ranging. For example, the promoter of a new railway or tramway scheme <u>may need compulsory powers</u> to buy land or to close streets. <u>A TWA order can grant these powers</u>.

The powers applied for must be relevant to the scheme. They may relate to matters that are necessary to support the scheme."

However, on a cautionary note, it is conceivable that the owner of any land being appropriated for <u>housing</u> development by utilisation of a TWA Act might have grounds to challenge that appropriation (*by use of a TWA*) and request that a "Section 226" mechanism be used; and if the land owners was successful with such a challenge (i.e. planning permission for houses was subsequently granted) then the enhanced land value would pass to the owner by way of compensation; and such would therefore utterly stymie the purpose of making the appropriation.

Hence; it would seem sensible, *pending legal advice*, to keep in mind that the use of a TWA might very likely have to be strictly confined to the *railway* element - including track-bed and platform locations (and car parking). TIPU* has been asked for clarification of this specific point but they have referred the author to seek specialist legal advice. The reader may contact:

* TIPU
Department for Transport
Great Minster House
33 Horseferry Road
London
SW1P 4DR

Telephone: 07971 145 887 or 07971 146 036
Email: transportinfrastructure@dft.gov.uk

Putting the TWA scheme into practice and appropriating land could affect people's enjoyment of their property and possibly also affect the environment. Because of this, applications for TWA orders have to follow a set procedure which allows people to give their views on the proposals:

Appropriation of land for the programme using a TWA.

The government website states:

"Compulsory purchase is a legal mechanism by which certain bodies (known as 'acquiring authorities') can acquire land without the consent of the owner. **Compulsory purchase powers can support the delivery of a range of development, regeneration and infrastructure projects in the public interest. In doing so, they can help to bring about improvements to social, economic and environmental wellbeing.**

Depending on the type of project that is being promoted, compulsory purchase powers may be granted through other legal instruments and there are separate sources of guidance on the procedures for those. The most commonly used are **orders under the Transport and Works**

Act 1992 authorising the construction and operation of guided transport projects (e.g. railways, tramways).

The process is as follows:

Preliminary enquiries
Acquiring authority considers whether land is required to deliver a project it is promoting and the extent of the land that may be required.

Negotiations to acquire by agreement

CPO preparation and submission
Acquiring authority formally 'resolves' to use its compulsory purchase powers and gathers detailed information about land ownership and occupation. The acquiring authority then makes the CPO, publicises it and submits it to the confirming authority.

Objecting to a CPO
Those affected by the CPO are invited to submit objections to the confirming authority.

CPO consideration
The CPO is considered by the confirming authority through a public inquiry or written representations.

Decision
The confirming authority decides whether to confirm, modify or reject the CPO.

Possession and acquisition
The acquiring authority takes ownership of the land.

Compensation
There is generally a right to compensation if your land is compulsorily acquired."

source: https://www.gov.uk/guidance/compulsory-purchase-and-compensation-guide-1-procedure

The Housing and Planning Act 2016

Where land has been acquired but existing easements obstruct the intended development purposes, the law allows such easements to be overridden. Section 203:

"203 Power to override easements and other rights

(5) Subsection (4) applies to the use of land in a case where—

(a) <u>there is planning consent</u> for that use of the land,

(b) the land has at any time on or after *[the relevant day]* —

> (i) become vested in or acquired by a specified authority or a specified company acting on behalf of a specified authority, or

> (ii) been appropriated by a local authority for planning purposes as defined by **section 246(1) of the Town and Country Planning Act 1990**,

(c) the authority could acquire the land compulsorily for the purposes of erecting or constructing any building, or carrying out any works, for that use, and

(d) the use is for purposes related to the purposes for which the land was vested, acquired or appropriated as mentioned in paragraph (b)."

Paragraph (5)(a) suggests that the necessity of having <u>prior planning permission</u> would similarly militate against the suitability of this Act for the purposes of appropriating land for the necessary housing development - in the same way that the 1990 Act does.

To the layman (including the author) the significance of the above Act is unclear; whether it is suited to the purposes of this proposal requires specialist legal advice, and no further comment is offered at this time.

It would also be essential that any intention to proceed with the making of planning applications for housing in rural areas would require specialist advice to ascertain that any variation from the National Planning Policy Framework predilection against rural house-building could be overcome. That is a matter outside this paper.

The author's conclusions in respect of the necessary legal framework for implementation of this project (were it to find favour generally) are as follows:

1. For acquisition by appropriation of land for the requisite <u>railway lines and associated infrastructure including (station) platforms</u> a TWA perfectly suits the case;

2. For the compulsory appropriation of land for the <u>housing element</u> of the project, the case is less clear:

     • it would seem that the 1990 Act, Section 226, is of doubtful value because of the 'planning value' transferring to the land owner - *as explained above*; and

     • the 2016 Act offers the same question as the 1990 Act;

3. Either the land <u>for housing</u> can be acquired under the appropriation powers of the TWA or it cannot. This may be an untested or relatively undefined aspect of the TWA law. Advice has been sought from the DoT / TIPU but no definitive reply has been provided at the time of publication other than to suggest taking specialist legal advice. *(any further clarification will be included in a subsequent edition).*

4. If a <u>TWA</u> *can* include powers of appropriation for a Housing land element (which is of great social benefit because of the affordable homes within the fundamental purpose of the proposal), then such by itself fully justifies the restoration of the railway lines.

5. If the TWA does **not** accord powers of appropriation for land <u>which has no planning permission for housing</u> (which is probably the case) *for the subsequent granting of such permission (for housing)* then **it becomes a case of negotiation with the land owner for the purchase of such land.**

6. In the case of such negotiation, the 'bargaining power' of the authority seeking to buy the land is significant because without the inclusion of the land within a project such as this that rural land is almost certainly never going to benefit from planning permission for rural housing <u>because of the NPPF predilection against it</u>; hence, the buyer can always look elsewhere for a more amenable seller. That will reflect in the negotiations in favour of a relatively lower purchase price for the land; **perhaps twice agricultural value would prove acceptable**. The seller would know that the primary purpose of the buyer acquiring the land would be to gain the uplift in value from a subsequent planning permission; hence, there would be no purpose in seeking a particularly or exceptionally high selling price because it becomes a major disincentive for the buyer, one which ultimately renders any purchase pointless. There is plenty of agricultural land out there and, unfortunately, a lot of struggling farmers willing to sell relatively tiny parcels of land.

7. Any action involving compulsory appropriation will always be at risk of legal challenge if there is the slightest doubt about the suitability and appropriate purpose of the mechanism used by the appropriating body; hence, for the purposes of acquisition of land for housing, price negotiation may likely prove to be the appropriate (and perhaps the only) mechanism. The very extensively distributed 1,000 homes per annum for 10 years suggests that relatively minor land parcels are all that would be required, and it likely could be purchased at prices which would not reflect the land value *with* planning permission for houses (as such would make the purchase pointless).

Opposition: mechanisms to overcome such

Appropriation is an unpleasant word, and an unwelcome process for those affected by it. The fairest possible compensation; indeed, generous such, will aid the public acceptance of compulsory acquisition of necessary land.

Many former stations along the closed branch lines were sold off and converted to residences. In a number of cases the recent debate about rail line restoration has left the owners of such properties in something of a quandary, in limbo, not knowing if any tangible rail restoration might ever eventuate; this puts a blight on the value of their property and a doubt about the viability of investing in home improvements *etc*.

Whilst **DaCSTaR** does not envisage that any restored station buildings would be of significant usefulness (low cost alternatives to the traditional *modus operandi* of former stations will be sought in each case), neither would the station building represent a generally accepted quality of home - with a dozen or more trains passing by so close each day. Hence all owners of former stations must be offered an equitable exit. This might be based on house price cost plus subsequent house-price inflation. Perhaps a generous margin might also be applied in recognition that such a sale might not have been the owner's preference (indeed, it might be compulsory).

Farmers will lose land (the former railway track-bed), but this is not of substantial land value; however, in each case consideration must be given to access to any land areas divided by a railway restoration. Topographical features, slopes, drainage and ground quality will be features to consider when contemplating such access alternatives. The detail is beyond the scope of this paper.

Local authorities might conceivably object in certain instances. Roads overlaid on former railway track-beds (and across former railway bridges) are the obvious example. It will be difficult to consider railway line diversions as the original engineers had a keen eye for the best possible option in order to minimise or avoid gradients; it will, from that perspective, be less of a challenge to re-route roads. A budget will therefore be required from the capital receipts fund to accommodate unavoidable highway changes.

Offices, factories and homes built on the former track-bed are instances which may represent the most challenging of obstacles; occupiers will be reluctant to concede the 'land take' which might be in very close proximity and which might create a nuisance or an inconvenience to them. *In extremis*, their whole property may require appropriation and compensation.

Perhaps for commercial properties the disruption could conceivably be substantial; however, the slow process of restoration of a railway line from A to B will certainly be a long one, and that should afford considerable notice to all affected property owners, suitably sufficient for alternatives to be procured with the assistance of the restoration capital fund.

The HS2 programme will offer examples of such processes.

HM Government support for railway restoration

The government has recognised that there is a case for the restoration of local or branch line railways. The following is a near *verbatim* excerpt from the HMG website:

"*Published in 1963, the Beeching Report was followed by the closure of almost 2,500 stations and around 5,000 miles of track. While most of the closures took place in the 1960s, some continued well into the 1970s. Many communities still remain isolated from the rail network following the closure of their local railway line or station more than 5 decades ago.*

"*Investing in transport links is essential to levelling up access to opportunities across the country, ensuring that communities are better connected, local economies flourish and more than half a century of isolation is undone.*

"*The Department for Transport launched a £500 million Restoring Your Railway Fund* in January 2020, to deliver on the government's manifesto commitment and start reopening lines and stations. MPs, local councils and community groups across England and Wales were invited to propose how they could use this funding to reconnect their local communities.*

* It must be born in mind that the government has also allocated £27 billion for road improvements; undoubtedly this is desirable and probably even necessary; however, it does put the projected spending of perhaps as much as £100 billion on HS2 in perspective; i.e. HS2 may benefit Birmingham and Manchester, but all other UK regions will get zero benefit from it, and the £500 million relative pittance for *Restoring your Railway* has actually now been axed.

"*The fund was split into 3 categories to support projects at different phases of development.*

1. The Ideas Fund

The Ideas Fund was set up to provide development funding for early-stage ideas to explore options to restore lost rail connections to communities.

There were 3 rounds of the Ideas Fund, with 141 unique bids received, sponsored by 210 MPs. Thirty-eight bids have received funding to develop a strategic outline business case.

2. Advanced Proposals

Advanced Proposals funding was established to support lines and stations already considered for restoration and those submitted to the fund that were beyond early development.

Advanced Proposals include the Dartmoor Line between Okehampton and Exeter, which officially reopened for year-round services on 20 November 2021, marking the first reopening under the programme.

3. The New Stations Fund

The New Stations Fund was launched to support proposals for new stations and the restoration of old station sites.

The New Stations Fund delivered 8 new stations across England and Wales since its inception in 2014. With Restoring Your Railway funding, 6 more are due to be delivered in 2024 and a further 2 proposals are being developed.

However; from November 2021, the Restoring Your Railway Fund is not accepting new proposals. The focus is now on realising the benefits of existing schemes to regenerate local economies and improve access to jobs, homes and education."

source:

https://www.gov.uk/government/collections/restoring-your-railway-fund

Contact: Restoringyourrailway@dft.gov.uk.

https://assets.publishing.service.gov.uk/government/uploads/system/uploads/attachment_data/file/1092282/restoring-your-railway-programme-update.pdf

The termination of acceptance of new proposals, unfortunately, represents something of a blow to aspirations of planned restoration of branch railways in the south-west; however, the very concept of the

DaCSTaR proposal is to fund *from within* the resources of the south-west counties and *not* to call on central government.

At the time of writing, the government has committed £98 billion to HS2. A cynical mind might conclude that a £500 million fund for "Restoring Your Railway" launched in 2020 (and stopped in 2022) against a £98 billion HS2 backcloth, was no more than a camouflage, a distraction, a sop to all those UK regions with no investment in railways at all. Indeed, and on a more positive, perhaps even optimistic, note, with the HS2 expenditure and project under increasingly negative scrutiny at a time of oncoming, imminent recession, conceivably the "Restoring Your Railway" fund itself might be restored so as to provide a more politically palatable exit route were HS2 to be axed.

A regional investment in **DaCSTaR** might conceivably become a welcome (small and much cheaper) substitute for HS2 for the government, an alternative in the strategy of 'levelling up', a boost to the regions, and a 'figleaf' to mitigate any embarrassment consequent to an axeing of HS2.

To promote such a notion, the proactive support of all south-west Members of Parliament would be significantly influential.

That the south-west peninsula of Devon and Cornwall is in need of a substantial boost to its economy is illustrated by the relative GDP values of its Districts within the UK as a whole, listed in the following table:

Gross domestic product per head by South-west District, 2020

UK £31,972

England £32,866

South West £28,012 (Devon and Cornwall)

Cornwall £21,154 *(is only 64% of the average for England)*

Devonshire £24,403 *(Devon County including Exeter, Plymouth and Torbay)*

of which

Exeter £43,783 *(is the most prosperous)*

all other regions are below the UK and England averages

South Hams £25,347

North Devon £25,239

Plymouth £23,877

East Devon £21,906

Teignbridge £19,533

Mid-Devon £18,763

Torbay £17,020

West Devon 16,778

Torridge £16,225 *(is the least prosperous, only 50.7% of the UK average and 49% of the average for England)*

Source:

https://www.ons.gov.uk/economy/grossdomesticproductgdp/bulletins/ regionaleconomicactivitybygrossdomesticproductuk/1998to2020

The Districts of Devon (and Somerset); **Cornwall** is a unitary authority.

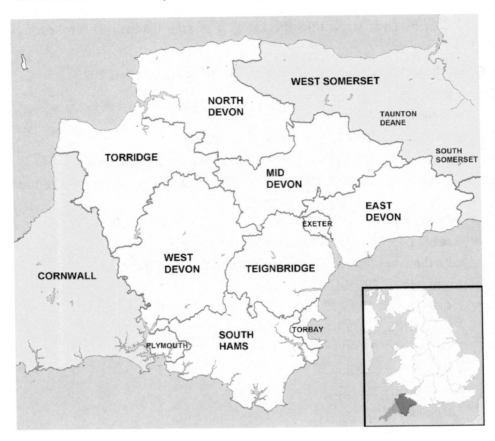

The area of *Cornwall* within this proposal is entirely within the former North Cornwall District (Local Authority).

Invitation: Contribute, correct, share, distribute, contact.

If you are a South-West Member of Parliament on either side of the House, please talk to your colleagues, particularly those with transport, housing and welfare briefs, about the potential interest for such a "TWA" Bill as would be required for this proposal.

If you are a County or District Councillor then, similarly, speak to your colleagues, both elected and officers, particularly those in transport, housing and welfare, to assess how such a proposal as this could aid you all to deliver on your obligations; and also discuss the implications with your local Planning Officers.

If you are a Parish Council representative, you might care to debate with your fellow councillors the merits and benefits that such a proposal as this could bring to your Parish, both in transportation and housing.

If you are a Planning Officer, doubtless the contents of this proposal will present some interesting considerations for you and your colleagues; the concepts within are unusual and may represent something of a challenge to orthodox thinking.

If you are involved with any of the present day efforts to stimulate **improved railways** for the region or to further develop the **heritage railways**, or even if you are just a railway 'buff', this proposal will doubtless spark interesting thought and speculation. Do give some time to considering how the ideas herein can aid your task.

If you are simply a member of the public and lamenting either the lack of affordable housing or rail links, please write to your MP and your local councils (whether County, District or Parish - or all of them) to express your conclusions after reading this proposal.

To everyone: whilst this proposal may, initially, lead you to a conclusion of "*It can't be done*", strive to think "outside the box", and begin again with the thought that the benefits would be immense to many tens of thousands of people; they are your neighbours (and they include voters); help them, and think "*How can it be done?*".

The author is working full-time in the tourism industry and is also an active author of historical fiction (*"The Continuing Voyages of HMS Surprise" series*); hence, the author is usually unavailable to discuss the contents of this proposal by telephone except by appointment.

Contact the author in the first instance by email at: **DaCSTaR.*uk@gmail.com***

Every reader, in whatever capacity that they may have read this proposal, is invited to comment on any aspect of it; indeed, everyone is invited to **contribute** to it, **even urged to do so**. Please contact the author at the above email address with anything useful you can add or correct.

The proposal is a 'rolling' one, envisaged to be an updated, incremental series of new editions as further information is added. This is merely **Edition One**.

It is planned to publish updated editions either on a monthly basis or as substantial additions are made, whichever seems most suitable.

If there is any content within this document which in any way inadvertently breaches copyright, please inform the author and it will be deleted.

DaCSTaR ® is a registered trademark belonging to the author.

All historical map excerpts are reproduced with the permission of the National Library of Scotland.

A number of informative national press articles and aerial photographs (some with superimposed routes for restored railway lines) have been reluctantly but unavoidably omitted as the author/publisher has no financial resources to fund licensing fees for such articles and photographs.

Reader contributions to meet such costs will be welcomed. The author intends to devote all net income from the sale of this book (expected to be very modest) towards such licensing costs in order that a successor edition can be more illustrative.

Appendix: Recommended books on the 'lost' railway lines of the region

The Taunton to Barnstaple Railway, a history of the Devon & Somerset Railway, in three volumes by Freddie Huxtable
simply magnificent in its scope and presentation; likely the best ever book on a former railway line; superlatives simply don't come close;

The North Devon Line by John Nicholas (The Tarka Line)
excellent,

The Ilfracombe Line by John Nicholas
a superb book,

Lines to Torrington by John Nicholas
the third in a wonderful trilogy,

The Exe Valley Railway including the Tiverton Branch by John Owen
first class,

North Devon Clay by Michael Messenger
a brilliant work,

The Branch Lines of Devon, by Colin G. Maggs
> **Plymouth, West & North Devon** and
> **Exeter, South, Central & East Devon**

Great books

Backtracking around... by Bernard Mills
> **Plymouth, Tavistock South & Launceston**
> **Plymouth, Callington, Tavistock North & The Southern Region main line to Okehampton**

Essential for a photographic glimpse of the present state of the lines

Lost Railways of Devon by Stan Yorke
well worthwhile reading

In the Tracks of the 'ACE', the destruction of the southern network west of Salisbury by Jeffery Grayer
A simply fabulous plethora of colour photos

Impermanent Ways... by Amyas Crump

    Volume 4 - Devon

    Volume 6 - Cornwall and West Devon

    Volume 14 Devon and Cornwall revisited

all three are a fascinating and illuminating present-day pictorial record in colour

Branch Line   **to Ilfracombe**

    to Padstow

    to Torrington

    to Lynton

    to Bude

    to Barnstaple

    to Launceston and Princetown

    to Tavistock

    around Bodmin

    around Tiverton including the Hemyock Branch

    All written by Vic Mitchell and Keith Smith

All of this series from Middleton Press are recommended as a concise and informative history of the lost branch lines

Railways of Devon and Cornwall by Anthony Burges

excellent black and white photographs; all with informative, detailed descriptions

North Devon's Lost Railways by Peter Dale

a slim volume with good B&W photos and brief statistics on each line

and

Devon's Railways by Helen Harris

Cornwall's Railways by Tony Fairclough

both small volumes are ideal starters for the subject

I tried to run a railway by Gerard Fiennes *is a greatly engaging book by an authoritative author who was contemporary with the "Beeching cuts". His second book* **Fiennes on Rails** *is very entertaining.*

Printed in Great Britain
by Amazon

21520117R00129